Fifty Hikes
in the Hudson
Valley

In spring, mountain laurel, kalmia latifolia, makes every walk delightful.

Fifty Hikes in the Hudson Valley

From the Catskills to
the Taconics, and
from the Ramapos
to the Helderbergs

**BARBARA McMARTIN AND
PETER KICK**

Photographs by the authors

Backcountry Publications
Woodstock,
Vermont

An Invitation to the Reader

Over time trails can be rerouted and signs and landmarks altered. If you find that changes have occurred on the routes described in this book, please let us know so that corrections may be made in future editions. The author and publisher also welcome other comments and suggestions. Address all correspondence to:

Editor, Fifty Hikes
Backcountry Publications, Inc.
P.O. Box 175
Woodstock, VT 05091

Library of Congress Cataloging in Publication Data

McMartin, Barbara.
  Fifty hikes in the Hudson Valley.

  Bibliography: p.17
  1. Hiking—Hudson River Valley (N.Y. and N.J.)—
Guide-books. 2. Hudson River Valley (N.Y. and N.J.)—
Description and travel—Guide books. I. Kick, Peter,
1951-   . II. Title.
GV199.42.H83M36   1985   917.47   85-1436
ISBN 0-942440-23-4

Second Printing, 1988, updated

Published by Backcountry Publications, Inc.
Woodstock, Vermont 05091

Printed in the United States of America

Text and cover design by Wladislaw Finne
Trail overlays by Richard Widhu

The map sections on pages 114, 118, 123, 129, 131, 136, 139, 143, 147, 150, 152, 157, 160, 164, 168, 170, 173, 176, 182, 184, 190, 195, 200, 203, and 211 are from "Catskill Trails," a five-map set published by the New York–New Jersey Trail Conference, © 1983. Reproduced by permission.

Pages 123, 125, 168, and 175 contain excerpts from *The Catskills from Wilderness to Woodstock* by Alf Evers; copyright © 1972 by Alf Evers; published by The Overlook Press, Lewis Hollow Road, Woodstock, New York 12498; $32.50.

Acknowledgments

While the hikes in this volume have been chosen for their scenic value, their selection was not only a matter of personal choice based on our experience; it also represents the favorites of regional experts, map-makers, hiking friends, and members of various clubs and organizations. Their advice was essential to our planning and writing.

Of those who helped to bring this guide to life, special thanks must be given to those friends who walked with us and shared their own love of nature with us. Thanks also is due to those whose special contributions were such an integral part of our project: W. Alec Reid, taking such care to print our photographs; Maurice Avery, James C. Dawson, Paul Leiken, Bleecker Staats, and Hugh Neil Zimmerman for reading parts of the work, hiking along with us, and helping to make sure that the written word corresponds accurately to the trails we enjoyed; Jack Karnig and Ray Donahue for background on trails; Justine L. Hommel, President of the Mountaintop Historical Society for access to archives and research material; the Huguenot Historical Society, the Dutchess Historical Society, and the very generous staffs of the Cold Springs, Newcastle, Haines Falls, and Olive Free Libraries; R. Laila Alberga, Elizabeth Kick, Eydie King, and Stephanie Steyer for typing.

Contents

Introduction

Southeastern New York State is dominated by the Hudson River, which flows past the wonders of its cities and industries. At the same time, the river touches some of the state's wilder lands, where the hiker can quickly escape the centers of civilization that dot the Hudson's banks. The wilderness at the Hudson's Adirondack headwaters needs no introduction. Some of the wild lands near the Hudson's southern cities are well-known, while others are almost undiscovered. This guide includes a variety of day hikes that will introduce you to the best of southeastern New York's wild lands not far from the Hudson.

The first visitors to the Hudson were mightily impressed by the rocklike fortresses of the Palisades, the rugged Hudson Highlands, and the mysteries of the distant blue Catskills. It is these rocky hills and mountains, bordering the Hudson, where most of the hikes described in this guide take place. The book will lead you to the northern Palisades, the Ramapos, the Highlands, the isolated lump of Schunemunk, the white cliffs of the Shawangunks, and the recesses of the distant Catskills. It reaches west to Delaware County, east to the Taconics, and north to the fortress of the Helderbergs. It brings you to the tops of this series of ranges which stand as if designed to give the best views of their succession and of the Hudson and Mohawk Valleys.

The History of the Rocks and Mountains

The drama of the southeastern New York landscape has a second story in the very rocks themselves. From the resistant limestones of the Helderberg Escarpment, to the dissected plateau of the Catskills, and into the crystalline Hudson Highlands lying beside the younger folded rocks of the Appalachians, you can see the parts of the puzzle that make up the region's geological history.

The largest geological province described in the guide is the Catskill region, occupying 1,500 square miles. Next to the Adirondacks, these are New York's highest and most rugged mountains and have the highest elevations. Slide Mountain (4,205 feet) is the highest peak and there are over a hundred other peaks with elevations over 3,000 feet in the Catskills. Three distinct regions—the escarpment (northeast), the southern, the central—define the Catskill plateau. There are several smaller topographic regions as well, many of which run east–west, or perpendicular to the southward movement of ice during the Pleistocene Age.

The profusion of streams that formed when the vast thickness of ice melted and retreated resulted in the erosion that produced the rugged character we see in the Catskills today. The plateau is drained to the north by the Schoharie Creek, a tributary of the Hudson via the

Mohawk. To the east, the Rondout, Esopus, and Kaaterskill rivers join the Hudson. To the south and west, the Delaware and Neversink rivers form the major drainages.

The rocks found in the Catskill plateau are relatively soft, consisting mainly of the sand and gravels deposited in the rivers and shallow seas of the Devonian Period, about 350 million years ago. These sands and gravels became the sandstones and conglomerates that have been uplifted and tilted. However, they have not been significantly folded, faulted, or changed by igneous and metamorphic activity. Thus they differ from many other mountain ranges such as the Appalachians or the Adirondacks.

The Catskills may have been a peneplain (almost a plain) at sea level before they were uplifted to their present elevation. The deep dissection (erosion) occurred when streams were rejuvenated during uplift. The resistant rocks remained, while the softer strata washed away. In some regions, joint patterns in the rock controlled erosion to produce the deep cloves (clefts) and wildly scenic hollows which steeped the Catskills in mystery and romance and contributed to the art and literary imagination of early America.

The uplift of the Devonian sediments took place in several stages and the Miocene and later stages were influenced by several episodes of Pleistocene glaciation. Today, the higher peaks are located where the uplift was greatest and where their conglomerate sandstones were able to resist erosion by the advance of the continental ice sheets and later by glacial melt waters.

What is perhaps most interesting about the underlying geology of the Catskills is the soil and hence the vegetation which flourishes there. The region represents the southernmost occurrence of boreal coniferous forests on glaciated uplands in North America. In contrast with this summit forest of spruce-fir and paper birch is the valley forest type, known as the Carolinian zone forest, which consists of oaks, hickories, occasional black birch, tulip trees, and, until recently, chestnut. According to Catskills ecologist Michael Kudish, "The proximity of the Carolinian and Canadian zones, especially in the eastern Catskills, together with the effects of man over two centuries, produces a rich, diverse flora, and creates a vegetation so complex that it nearly defies explanation."

While they are unique floristically and geologically, the Catskills have yet another distinguishing characteristic: their youth. All the surrounding ranges are considerably older. To the east lie the 450 million-year-old Taconics, formed during a continental collision that displaced older sediments in a period called the Taconic Orogeny.

South of the Catskills are the Shawangunks, and although they are close to the Taconics in age, their evolution is more related to the Catskills. Extensive sands and quartz-rich gravels were deposited in a shallow sea during the Silurian Period, about 450 million years ago. Much later, the resulting sandstones and conglomerates were uplifted and differentially eroded.

The Hudson Highlands to the south are a series of granitic and metamorphic rocks. They were intruded and metamorphosed at great depth over a billion years ago. Later, about 450 million years ago, during the Taconic Orogeny, the rocks were folded, faulted, and uplifted to their present form.

Hiking in Southeastern New York

By combining walks in these geologically interesting mountains—the best of the east coast's scenery, in our opinion—with a few walks in the Hudson Valley itself, this guide offers the hiker an excellent range of opportunities.

For residents of southern New York State, the special appeal of most of these trails is their proximity to New York City. The majority of the trailheads lie within two hours of the city.

There are two ways to enjoy these walks. The social hikers will find many walking groups that offer regularly scheduled hikes and trips. The New York–New Jersey Trail Conference will put you in touch with many of them. Groups such as the Catskill 3500 Club, the Appalachian Mountain Club, and chapters of the Adirondack Mountain Club all offer outing schedules for a variety of hikers. Each organization also fills a second role by providing mechanisms for the hiker to return something to the land. With programs of trail maintenance, conservation, planning to prevent overuse, and education to promote wise use, these organizations help protect our wild lands.

Those who seek quiet in the wild lands also can find that. Some of these routes are never heavily used. Others are, but, even here, early spring and late fall trips will mix solitude with expanded vistas in ways sure to please any wilderness seeker.

There are relatively few hikes on the east side of the Hudson. Its gentler hills were settled early, and although the farms are shrinking, the settlements have grown to fill most of the open land. In contrast, the forests on the west side of the Hudson have been preserved as the valley's water source and as part of the New York State Forest Preserve, whose unique state constitutional protection ensures they will remain "forever wild." Lands within the Blue Line of the Catskill Park offer the largest group of hikes in this guide.

Almost all the lands traversed by today's trails were once settled and used by farmers, miners, loggers, and romantics. Their presence inevitably is reflected in the lore that surrounds the trails, and we explore that history as well as the natural scene. While this guide serves as an invitation to the mountain ranges and valleys of the southern part of the state, it cannot even begin to probe the vast history that enlivens each route. For further information, consult the bibliography at the end of this introduction.

Before You Start

There is an enormous range of hikes in this guide, from easy strolls to strenuous climbs. The information about distance, time, and elevation change should help you gauge the difficulty of each hike and your preparedness. Almost all follow clearly marked trails, although this can change. The greatest source of confusion seems to be the constant revisions in trail designation for the more southerly trails, where interconnecting routes can be confusing and color changes in the markings are in progress.

The area offers many more walks than are described in this book, and references to some of the best of the other guides are given in the bibliography. In order to discover other hikes, or to become better prepared for outdoor adventures, you may wish to join one of the hiking groups listed at the end of the introduction.

Preparedness is key to your enjoyment, and you should be well equipped before you start. This should include beginning to understand the use of map and compass to complement the information in this guide. If you are new to hiking, it is definitely a good idea to join a hiking group and learn from those with experience. The more background you have in the woods, the greater will be your safety as well as enjoyment. Do not count on the following summary of what you need to know to prepare you for every situation you are likely to encounter. While this guide includes excursions for all ranges of experience, this introduction is not a primer for beginning hikers. Treat it instead as a checklist and a set of reminders.

The Weather

Whenever possible, wait for a sunny day. The pleasures are much greater and the problems more predictable. But even on sunny days you should be prepared for changes and extremes. It can be twenty or more degrees colder on the mountaintops of the Catskills than in the nearby Hudson Valley. Storms can appear on short warning.

Because if often can be too hot in summer for strenuous hikes, there are many who prefer walking in southern New York State in fall and spring, and these are the most changeable times. Extremes from heat waves to snowstorms can occur. But the rewards of fewer people and the expanded distant vistas in the leafless season makes it all worthwhile.

Preparations

Even with the best of forecasts, your watchword should be *plan for the unexpected*. Possible changes in temperature means you should take extra clothing, especially rain gear. Experiment with layers of light waterproof gear. Certainly in the mountains you will want a layer of wool, even if in summer it is only a sweater in your daypack. Places to swim are mentioned, so take along a bathing suit (if you want one).

Many of the trails are as smooth as a sidewalk; some are as rubble-filled as a rock pile. For most of these hikes a sturdy pair of well-broken-in, over-the-ankle boots is essential. The new lightweight Gore-Tex or similar material boots are wonderful; they give good traction and support, and they are all you need except on the higher mountain trails in early spring or winter. You will want to wear two pairs of socks, an inner lightweight pair and a heavy outer pair that is at least partly wool.

Of course you will carry a sturdy daypack, large enough to hold your lunch and a few necessities. The separate pouch along the side of our packs always contain a whistle, a case with dry matches, a jackknife, a small can opener, chapstick, and a space blanket. We have used them all.

Carry a map and compass, a flashlight in case you are delayed beyond dusk, and a watch so you do not panic if that happens. You also need a small first aid kit, containing a few bandages, first aid cream, and moleskin for the unexpected blister.

Take along a small squeeze bottle of insect repellent, one that contains "deet" (Ndiethylmetatoluamide). There are black flies in early spring, although not the legions that endure so long in the Andirondacks. Fill a zip-lock bag with toilet paper and throw in a few "wash and dries" to use before lunch on those dry mountaintops.

All wise hikers are likely to carry these basic items, but it is strongly recommended as well that you wear a pair of unbreakable glasses—light tinted sunglasses even if you require no prescription. It is all too easy to run into an overhanging branch or twig.

You will enjoy the hikes more if you carry binoculars and learn to watch for birds. Besides, binoculars are essential for identifying distant sights. A small magnifying glass can add to your discoveries of nature. You may even enjoy carrying a small, lightweight altimeter that works according to barometric pressure. On relatively steady days, it is a good clue to progress on a mountain; on unstable days, it can alert you to sudden changes in the weather.

Of course, you should always carry water when you hike. These mountains are really dry much of the year, and few springs exist. It is becoming increasingly dangerous to trust open water sources because of the spread of *giardia*. And, remember to take enough water. Dehydration on summer days is quite possible; it can even happen on a sunny leafless spring day or in winter. Those lightweight fuel bottles of durable aluminum with deep screw tops are wonderful for carrying liquids, but to avoid confusion their contents should be clearly marked.

Remember, hiking should be fun. If you are uncomfortable with the weather or tired, turn back and make the complete hike another day. Do not create a situation where you risk yourself or your companions.

And, never walk alone. Be sure someone knows your intended route and expected return time. Always sign in at the DEC trailhead registers where they are available. The unexpected can occur. Weather can change, trail markings can become obscured, you can fall, and you can get lost. But, you will not be in real danger if you have anticipated the unexpected.

Behavior in the Woods

So, now you are safe in the woods, but what about the woods? The environment that may threaten you can be just as fragile as you are, and you are the only one who can protect it.

Leave no sign of your presence. Use pit privies if they are available. If they are not, bury your wastes at least 200 feet from water or from a trail or path. None of these trips requires camping, but there are several where overnight trips are possible. When you camp, do not bathe with soap in lakes or streams; when picnicking or camping, carry wash water as well as dish water back from the shore. Keep lakes or running water pure. If you are camping, carry a stove for cooking, and do not build fires unless they are needed. In most of the parks, fires are prohibited. These are very fire-prone areas. If you need to build a fire on a Catskill hike, for instance, build it on dry stones, gravel or sandy soil surfaces, surrounded by a fire ring to protect duff, leaf mold, or organic soils from burning. Remember, only dead and down wood can be used.

Respect the rights of others and help preserve natural areas for future hikers.

Notes for Using this Guide

Summaries at the beginning of each hike list the hiking distance, vertical rise, time on the trail, and the United States Geological Survey (USGS) topographical map (or maps) or the New York–New Jersey Trail Conference trail map for the area the hike traverses. Unless otherwise noted, distances are for the round trip or circuit. Distances are given from state markers where they are available and correct (incorrect signs are noted in some instances). Where measured mileage information has not been available, distances have been computed from the USGS and are correct to within 10 percent.

Vertical rise refers to the total change in cumulative elevation for the hike. In cases where the terrain is relatively level, a numerical figure has not been used.

Hiking time is given for the total time at a leisurely pace, but it is simply the minimum needed to walk the trail as described. The text often tells you to allow more time for sightseeing.

Most of the hikes in this book are accompanied by sections taken from the topographic map (or maps) mentioned at the beginning of each hike description, so it is not essential to have an entire map with you on the trail. These maps, however, do give the larger picture and you will have more fun on a mountain top if you can identify some of the surrounding countryside. A cautionary note on the USGS maps: while contours and elevations are by and large reliable, some of the man-made features, including trails, are seriously out of date. The New York State Department of Transportation 7.5' quadrangles, which correspond in area and name to the USGS quads, tend to have more recent planimetric information, but they have the disadvantage of being printed in only two colors (USGS maps are in four colors). Approximately half of the hikes in this book are accompanied by small sections of the "Catskills Trails" maps, a five-map set published in 1983 by the New York–New Jersey Trail Conference. The maps in this series are far more convenient and up-to-date than either the USGS or Department of Transportation quads, and we recommend acquiring them (see page 16). With the exception of Mohonk (#21), all hikes using a topo base map have a trail overlay, and—in the case of loop hikes—arrows showing the direction of travel. A few of the hikes are in state parks, and for reasons of scale, a sketch map instead of a topo base map has been provided for #17 (Olana).

If you do not know how to read a map, you should learn to do so before hiking all but about a dozen of the simplest trails in this guide. Spend time walking with someone who does know how to read a map. The same instructions are appropriate for the use of a compass. You may not need either on the easiest of this guide's trails, but walking the easier routes with map and compass will allow you to become comfortable with their use, so you can extend your hikes be-

yond the ones described, or to more difficult hikes.

Other Helpful Information

The New York State Department of Environmental Conservation (DEC)
50 Wolf Road
Albany, NY 12233
The DEC, through its Division of Lands and Forests, manages the State Forest Preserve lands of the Catskills and detached parcels of state land outside the Catskills. The DEC is responsible for Search and Rescue, planning for management, supervision of campsites, and issuing of camping permits. (Unless expressly prohibited, campers may stay for up to three nights in one location on state land without a permit and may apply for a permit for longer stays.) The DEC also publishes regional sketch-type trail maps. It is easiest to obtain local information from one of the regional offices listed below.

DEC Region 3 Headquarters
23 South Putt Corners Road
New Paltz, NY 12561
914-255-5453

DEC Region 4 — Lands and Forests
Sub-Office
Jefferson Road
Stamford, NY 12167
607-652-7364

DEC Region 4 — Lands and Forests
Sub-Office
439 Main Street
Catskill, NY 12414
518-943-4030

Taconic State Park and Recreation
Commission
Mills–Norrie State Park
Staatsburg, NY 12580
914-889-4100
The Taconic State Park and Recreation Commission manages land assigned to

The trail to Kaaterskill High Peak

the Office of Parks and Recreation on the east side of the Hudson. It is responsible for supervising trail maintenance there, including the Hudson Highlands.

Palisades Interstate Park Commission
Bear Mountain, NY 10091
914-786-2701 or 212-562-8688
The PIPC issues permits and trail information and supervises Harriman and Bear Mountain State Parks and the state land of the Shawangunks.

Mohonk Preserve, Inc. and Mohonk Mountain House
Mohonk Lake
New Paltz, NY 12561
Preserve: 914-255-0919
The Mohonk Preserve supervises access to preserve lands, provides a map to preserve lands when the access fee is paid, publishes a brief natural history of the Shawangunks, and manages the preservation of this unique natural resource.

New York–New Jersey Trail Conference
GPO Box 2250
New York, NY 10116
212-696-6800
The Conference coordinates the construction and maintenance of some 800 miles of hiking trails, including the Appalachian Trail in New York and New Jersey, and the Long Path, which connects the metropolitan area with the Catskills. They also publish regional maps of the Catskills, the Hudson Highlands, Harriman Park, the South Taconics, and the Shawangunks. They are co-sponsors and editors of the *New York Walk Book,* the most comprehensive guide of its kind to the greater metropolitan area. Small sections of their "Catskills Trails" maps have been reproduced in this book, and the entire five-map set may be purchased from the conference for $9.95 plus 90¢ for postage and handling (New York state residents should add sales tax). Some 70

hiking clubs and conservation organizations belong to the conference, along with 5,000 individual members. Applications for individual membership are invited, and the $15 annual fee includes, among other things, a subscription to the *Trailwalker.* This bi-monthly publication describes the activities of the member clubs and features timely articles, book reviews, and trail updates. It is a reliable source of information on trail closings, relocations, and other potential problems associated with the hikes described in this book.

Appalachian Mountain Club

New York City office: 24 East 38th Street, NY, NY 10016
212-684-3683
The AMC helps build and maintain trails in southern New York, including some sections of the Appalachian Trail and trails in Harriman and Hudson Highlands State Parks. The AMC is also a leader in conservation, canoeing and bicycling in the metro area. For the area covered by this book, they have a Catskill Chapter and a New York/North Jersey Chapter.

Chapters of the Adirondack Mountain Club

174 Glen Street
Glens Falls, NY 12801
518-793-7737
The ADK can supply information about their Ramapo, North Jersey, Mid-Hudson, Mohican, Albany, and Schenectady Chapters, all of which schedule regular hikes in the area described in this guide. Membership is currently $30 a year.

The Catskill 3500 Club
C/o Cyrus Whitney
41 Morley Drive
Wyckoff, NJ 07481
The Club is primarily a hiking organization. Candidate members receive notices

of trips and outings. A membership patch is given for completing climbs of 34 summits over 3500 feet, of which four from a specified list must be climbed in winter.

The Catskill Center for Conservation and Development, Inc.
Arkville, NY 12406
914-586-2611
The Catskill Center is a regional advocate for land use planning and environmental management, and is active in natural area preservation, historic preservation, community revitalization and public review of regionally significant projects. It publishes general interest books and technical studies as well as a newsletter on conservation issues affecting the Catskills. The center also publishes a map entitled "The Catskill Region." Offices are in the Erpf House on Route 28 at Arkville, and applications for membership are welcome.

The Nature Conservancy, New York Field Office
1736 Western Avenue
Albany, NY 12203
The Conservancy manages and protects natural areas throughout the United States. Two hikes in this guide are in Conservancy preserves.

Map Information Unit,
New York State Department of Transportation
State Campus, Bldg. 4, Room 105
Albany, NY 12232
518-457-4408
The state publishes and sells a variety of maps, including topo maps based on the USGS quadrangles.

Branch of Distribution, US Geological Survey
Box 25286, Denver Federal Center
Denver CO 80225
Most sporting goods stores and a few other retailers in the metropolitan area sell USGS maps, but for the occasional one that is unavailable, it is good to be able to order from the source.

Bibliography

Adams, Arthur G. *The Hudson through the Years.* Westwood, NJ: Lind Publications, 1983.

Bedell, Cornelia F. *Now and Then and Long Ago in Rockland County.* New York: Arno Press, Historical Society of Rockland County, 1941.

Cole, The Rev. David. *History of Rockland County.* New York: J. B. Beers & Co., 1884.

De Lisser, Richard Lionel. *Picturesque Ulster County.* Kingston, NY: Styles and Bruyn Publishing Co., 1896.

Evers, Alf. *The Catskills from Wilderness to Woodstock.* Woodstock, NY: The Overlook Press, 1982. Reprint of 1972 Doubleday edition with additions.

Goldring, Winifred. *Guide to the Geology of John Boyd Thacher Park (Indian Ladder Region) and Vicinity.* Albany: New York State Museum Handbook 14, 1933.

Haring, H. A. *Our Catskill Mountains.* New York: G. P. Putnam's Sons, 1931.

The Hemlock (Catskill Center News). Co-sponsored publication of the Catskill Center and the Mountain Top Historical Society. Box 263, Haines Falls, NY, 1980.

Hoffer, Audrey and Elizabeth Mikols. *Unique Natural Areas in the Catskill Region.* Arkville, NY: Catskill Center for Conservation and Development, Inc., 1974.

Hopkins, E. M. *The Sunk Mine.* May 1887. Copied by Olive Adams, Nelsonville, June 1957, papers in the library of the Putnam County Historical Society.

Kudish, Michael. *Vegetational History of the Catskill High Peaks.* Doctoral dissertation, State University College of Forestry, Syracuse University, 1971.

Laird, J. R. Dunham. "Dunderberg," in *South of the Mountain.* Vol. 8, No. 4. Tappan Zee Historical Society, October-December, 1964.

Longstreth, T. Morris. *The Catskills.* New York: The Century Co., 1918.

Lossing, Benson J. *The Hudson: From Wilderness to the Sea.* Facsimile of the 1866 edition. Somersworth, NH: New Hampshire Publishing Company, 1972.

MacCracken, Henry Noble. *Old Dutchess Forever!* New York: Hastings House Publishers, 1956.

Mack, Arthur C. *Enjoying the Catskills.* New York: Funk and Wagnalls Co., 1950.

Mylod, John. *Biography of a River: The People and Legends of the Hudson Valley.* New York: Hawthorne Books, Inc., 1969.

New York–New Jersey Trail Conference, *New York Walk Book,* New York: Doubleday, 1984.

Newman, Joseph. "Recollections," in *South of the Mountain,* Vol. 13, No. 1. Historical Society of Rockland County, January-March, 1969.

O'Brien, Raymond J. *American Sublime: Landscape and Scenery in the Lower Hudson Valley.* New York: Columbia University Press, 1981.

Posselt, Eric. *The Rip Van Winkle Trail, A Guide to the Catskills.* New York: Storm Publishers, 1952.

Putnam County Historical Society, *The Last 100 Years.* Third Workshop, 1957.

Quinn, Louise Hasbrouck, The Rev. A. Elwood Corning, Joseph W. Emsley, and Willet C. Jewell. *Southeastern New York: A History of Ulster, Dutchess, Orange, Rockland and Putnam.* New York: Lewis County Publishing Company, Inc., 1946, Vol. II, p. 942 ff.

Ransom, James M. *Vanishing Ironworks of the Ramapos.* New Brunswick, NJ: Rutgers University Press, 1966.

Reed, John. *The Hudson Valley.* New York: Bonanza Books, 1960.

Rockwell, The Rev. Charles. *The Catskill Mountains and the Region Around.* New edition. Cornwall, NY: Hope Farm Press, 1973.

Snyder, Bradley. *The Shawangunk Mountains: A History of Nature and Man.* New York: The Mohonk Preserve, Inc., 1981.

Van Zandt, Roland. *The Catskill Mountain House.* New Brunswick, NJ: Rutgers University Press, 1966.

Van Zandt, Roland, *Chronicles of the Hudson: Three Centuries of Travelers' Accounts.* New Brunswick, NJ: Rutgers University Press, 1971.

Legend for "Catskill Trails" Maps

Marked Trail and Terminus . . . . ➜

Trail Name and Color . . . . **DP(R)**
See reverse for Trail name and description
Trail Color
(R) — Red **(B)** — Blue **(Y)** — Yellow

Unmarked Trail . . . . – – – –

Parking . . . .●**P**

Viewpoint . . . . ★

Leanto . . . .●**L**

Water (Spring) . . . . ●**W**

New York State   Forest Preserve
Forest Preserve Lands . . . . ▨▨▨▨
                              Private Land

Keep Out (private land) . . . . **KO**

Marked elevation . . . . △*4040*

Unmarked elevation . . . . ×*3810*

Primary Road . . . . ▬▬▬

Secondary Road . . . . ▬▬▬

Route Markers (State, County) . . . 214 16

Bus Stop . . . .●**B**

Southern
Hudson
Valley

1

The Hook

Distance: 11.7 miles
Time: 6 hours
Vertical rise: 1,200 feet
Maps: USGS 7½′ Haverstraw; USGS 7½′ Nyack

The towering cliffs of the Hook have awed travelers to southern New York State for centuries. Henry Hudson and the sailors who followed made note of this impressive headland as they made their way up the Hudson. The man-made cliffs of abandoned quarries further etch the skyline into sheer red-brown walls that appear to continue the Palisades. Whether walking to the high point in spring or fall to watch the hawk migration or bicycling along the paths that hug the shores, you will find much to enjoy in the parklands run by the Palisades Interstate Park Commission that stretch from Nyack to Haverstraw on the Hudson's western shore.

A portion of the Long Path takes the high route from Nyack across the Hook and the hills called the Seven Sisters. With a bit of bushwhacking, you can make a circuit walk along the hills and back on the shore path, enjoying the best of views of woods and water. Probably you will find it best to leave a car at either end, however, as the southern ends of the two portions are not connected easily on foot, and any connection involves crossing private lands.

Leave your return car at Nyack State

The Hook

Park at the end of Broadway in Nyack. Go back south on Broadway to Birchwood Avenue, then west to NY 9W. Drive north on 9W, and as you leave the village, just beginning to climb the hill behind the Hook, you will see a place to park on the west side of the road. There is another turnout at the crest of the hill, from which you can walk back to the trailhead. The trail, marked with turquoise blazes, begins on the east side of the road, a little north of the first turnout.

A fifteen-minute walk brings you to the top of the Hook with views toward New York City and north to the quarry behind Rockland Lake. Beyond the quarry lies the massif of Dunderberg that ends in the Timp. Farther north and on the other side of the river lies the ragged contour of Breakneck Ridge leading up toward South Beacon. The river, wide here at Tappan Bay, is pinched to the north by Croton Point. Farther north, it opens out into its widest segment at Haverstraw Bay before becoming choked into the narrows of the Hudson Highlands.

You are standing on the 736-foot peak of the Verdrietege, or tedious headland, so-called by early Dutch sailors who struggled to sail upwind around it. But the landscape at your feet is not what the Dutch sailors saw, and the history of that

Long Clove
ROAD
Light
o

0   0.5   1.0 mile

N

HOOK

MOUNTAIN

VERDRIETEGE
STATE

303

CONRAIL

Swartwout Lake
146

Golf

Course

East

Gethsemane
Cem

Congers
BM 191

Br

Trough Hol

Sewage
Disposal

ongers

173

Congers Lake
137

ROCKLAND
LAKE

ROCKLAND LAKE
Rockland Lake
148

STATE PARK

Romie
Sch
232
BM

HIGHWAY

Hackensack R

9w

Hook

Mountain

622

HOOK

KINGS

St Pauls
Sch

ROAD

Sewage
Disposal

Lake Road
Sch   169

303

RIDGE

Golf

Uppe
Cliff

348

Br

AY

Course

303

HOOK MOUNTAIN
STATE PARK

Hook Mtn

End P

Marydell
Camp

P Start

landscape accounts for a good portion of the preservation movement that resulted in the parks now lining the Hudson's shores.

The Palisades' traprock, diabase that is volcanic in origin, here surfaces through the base of Triassic sandstone and shale Quarries along the river to the south were active in the 1820s, and the columnar cliffs of the Hook were quarried extensively in the 1870s and 1880s with the introduction of dynamite and heavy earth-moving equipment. The basalt columns were crushed for traprock for macadam roads and later in the 1890s for concrete for Manhattan buildings. Angered at first only by the ear-shattering explosions heard up and down both sides of the river, residents of both New York and New Jersey began to speak out against the quarries. It was not until 1894 that a well-organized group opposed the visual desecration of the cliffs the quarrying caused.

Finally, in 1900, after several years of legislative debate, which was fueled by the argument "that preservation would largely benefit those who enjoyed the view from the New York side of the Hudson," a study commission report was accepted. It called for a permanent interstate park commission and the acquisition of land along the Palisades for recreational purposes. With both private and public funds, the acquisition program progressed from acquiring lands from the top of the cliff face to the river to adding clifftop lands north to Nyack. The Hook was still threatened until the Palisades Interstate Park was extended northward in 1906. By 1915 all of the Hook was acquired by the Palisades Interstate Park Commission.

The clifftop trail continues north through Hook Mountain Park by first heading down the incredibly narrow and sinuous ridge. Trees block the views here, but you will climb a handful of open summits before the day is over. One opening discloses Rockland Lake and the landing from which the lake's ice was shipped to New York City. A forty-minute walk brings you into a valley and shortly beyond the second hill with several view spots on its summit.

The descent from this hilltop is marked by a left fork that takes you across an old roadway that once led toward Rockland Landing. Beyond the low point another roadway comes in from the left. As you start to climb, you will be amazed at the amount of rock work that was used to construct these old roadways, making an especially lovely base for the trail to follow. Gentle ups and downs follow. The curved stone wall and old foundation beside the trail are sure to intrigue you.

As you begin to climb again, about an hour and forty minutes into the trip, watch for a path up to the right to a promontory overlooking Croton Point, unquestionably one of the best views of the day.

This is a good place to observe the clues to the second major industry of the region's past, clues that are much less obvious than those of the quarries. At the shore below you are the remains of old docks, the successors to Slaughter's Landing, a settlement begun in 1711 by John Slaughter from Rockland Lake. An ice business was started at Rockland Lake in 1831 when Moses G. Leonard impressed New York City hotelkeepers with the cleanliness and purity of the lake's ice. In 1855, the business became the Knickerbocker Ice Company, the largest in New York, employing as many as 1,000 men. Ice was cut from the lake and stored for shipment south to New York City. It was moved from the lake via an endless conveyor cable to the landings, where three pairs of tracks led across the docks whose ruins are guarded by an old lighthouse. Four hundred ton loads were carried south on barges.

Returning to the trail, within a few feet you meet what appears to be a trail intersection. The way right is steep and unmarked. Turn left for an almost equally steep descent, behind a row of houses and old foundations, and out to a road that could provide an alternate trailhead for a portion of this walk. This point also can be reached by car from Rockland State Park, which is to your left (west). Rockland Landing is on the waterfront to your right. The three-mile walk to this point along the summits should take just over two hours.

Immediately north of the stanchions that bar vehicular traffic into the park, the turquoise-marked trail continues, first passing an early nineteenth century cemetery. The first hilltop with a view is scarcely five minutes from the road, a perch atop the first in the string of smaller quarries north of the landing. Just beyond, in spring you will be amazed to see Dutchman's-breeches blooming only a short distance from the prickly pear cactus that seems to enjoy this dry location. The trail continues on the west side of the ridge, emerging to a series of more or less obscure views, depending on the season. At one spot, you look down on red-brown cliffs and pine seedlings that are filling in a second quarry.

The trail descends, turns left past a filtration plant, and heads up the next ridge bordered by vine-covered stone walls. For a short time the trail follows the park boundary. Just beyond, a side trail, right, leads to a lookout with spectacular views atop a third quarry. A series of gentle ups and downs ends in a sharp, short drop into a hemlock-filled valley. Immediately you emerge with views to the north and northwest. The next downhill leads off the ridge.

The way out of the small valley is viewless, its taller trees making the segment feel like a remote woodland trail where the roller coaster effect of the ridge continues for a delightful forty-five-minute walk. There is one summit that yields views of narrow DeForest Lake. As the trail turns sharply east and steeply down toward the river almost above the railroad tunnel, you feel suspended above the water. The hemlock-covered bank parallels the shore, 400 feet above it. The trail descends along the ridge, then lies exposed beneath power lines where you have a view of Stony Point beyond Haverstraw Bay. You see an old bridge and a roadway and could turn right to an alternate trailhead with limited parking at the junction of NY 304 and 9W. This point is 3.2 miles from Rockland Landing Road. Your trek from the Hook across the hills of the Seven Sisters—and surely twice that number of small knobs and crests—has taken about four hours.

Unfortunately, without walking into Haverstraw, there is no good way to cross to the waterside trail. You can turn right and walk north for 0.3 mile, first heading down the roadway and out to the railroad line. Cross it, after being certain no trains are around, and walk north along the tracks to find an easy descent to the waterside path. Here bicyclists, joggers, and strollers will join you for the return, but the lack of privacy does not detract from the pleasant route. The level 5.2 miles back to Nyack State Park are walked easily in two hours, unless you stop to examine the quarries en route.

Note: If you find the parking lot on 9W closed, drive 0.9 mile north to the southern entrance to Rockland State Park. In winter, turn right, then park in 0.3 mile at the gate to the Executive Golf Course and walk 0.3 mile uphill to the turning loop. In season, drive to the parking area, but park away from the club house. A yellow-marked trail heads east from the turning loop. It winds uphill, passing a small pond in 0.2 mile. In another 200 yards, it intersects the blue trail in a draw on the ridge, less than 0.4 mile north of the summit of Hook Mountain. Turn right and pass two small lookouts on the 160-foot climb to the summit.

The Southern Ledges
of Bear Mountain State Park

Distance: 6.5 miles
Time: 6 hours
Vertical rise: 1,000 feet
Map: USGS 7½' Sloatsburg; NY–NJTC Harriman–Bear
  Mtn., #3

The Ramapo Mountains run from northern New Jersey into Rockland and Orange counties. Their eroded slopes have risen above nearby seas for nearly 600 million years, making them among the oldest land masses on the continent. These mountains are part of the Reading Prong, which extends from Reading, Pennsylvania, to the Hudson Highlands and north to the Green Mountains of Vermont. This Precambrian formation is the result of periods of intense folding and metamorphism of sediments deposited more than a billion years ago and of intrusions of magma that occurred several times in the Precambrian era. While these forces leave a complicated picture for the geologist, later events, the Ice Ages, are much clearer. The striations and polished rocks and the ubiquitous erratics are obvious to the hiker on any walk through the Ramapos.

Whether the name Ramapo derives from an Indian name for the potholes that mark the Ramapo River, or whether it comes from a Leni–Lenape word that means "place of slanting rock" is not known. The latter is certainly more descriptive, for the views of uplifted faces of various metamorphosed layers are also a part of each hike.

Bear Mountain and Harriman State Parks span most of the Ramapos in New York State. Their origins are curious. In 1908 the State proposed to build a state prison at Bear Mountain. Among the many who protested this desecration of beautiful and historic lands was Mrs. Edward H. Harriman, widow of the railroad tycoon, who offered to give the Palisades Interstate Park Commission 10,000 acres, the nucleus of the modern parks. In return it was agreed that the Commission's jurisdiction would be extended north along the Hudson, and plans for the prison would be dropped. Subsequent gifts and purchases have enlarged the park to its present 51,000 acres and allowed for scenic parkways and the building of dams to create or enlarge the numerous bodies of water that dot the park.

The parks are managed now for the hordes of people from the metropolitan area who enjoy the ski-jumping, skating, waterfronts and picnicking in the more developed areas. It is often difficult to escape the crowds, but it can be done. There is a dense honeycomb network of trails that cover almost every mountain top and follow every handsome stream. This wonderful network, built over a period of many years by hikers and club groups of the NY–NJ Trail Conference, also can be a problem to those unfamiliar with the park. It is difficult to know how to combine these segments into interesting loops, convenient to places where parking is permitted. The four walks described in Harriman State Park help solve both these problems, although it is still recommended that a hiker seeking a measure of solitude walk in the off-season or during the week if possible. There are extensive rules about parking and disturbing flora and fauna, prohibitions against fires, and limits to the use of shelters. Walking on the left side of the road is permitted, but only during the week. Winter hikers must register at Police Headquarters at the Administration Building at Bear Mountain, and those with additional questions about park use should check in there as well.

A walk along the southern ledges of Harriman State Park does a great job of taking you away from the crowds. It is a loop from the parking area adjacent to the Beaver Meadow Nature Center, which is less than two miles northeast from the park boundary on Seven Lakes Parkway. Behind the center in the field near Stony Brook, you will find two trails. Start on the Reeves Brook Trail, marked with three white dots. It heads gently uphill away from Stony Brook to follow its tributary. It winds for a mile gently uphill and down, passing a rock-tumbled ravine, skirting a swamp, passing handsome rock ledges and outcrops. Just over half an hour will bring you to a four-way intersection.

The white trail goes straight ahead, a blue trail forks left 0.1 mile for a detour to Pulpit Rock, which crowns the boulder-strewn hillside to the south. For the loop, take the right fork, a fainter foot path than the rest, to the Seven Hills Trail marked with a blue square on a white ground square. Within ten minutes you

gain a view west over the Ramapo Valley.

Beyond this overlook, called Torne View, you descend into a draw just below the saddle between two hills and begin to climb a rocky path on the rubble-filled hillside that ends in a scramble up to the intersection with the white marked HTS, Hillburn Torne Sebago Trail. This last section checks out at about three-quarters of a mile, but the rough walking may make you take more than half an hour. Just off the trail on the ledge above you is an overlook with views south to New York City. Also at this intersection, you could detour south along the joint HTS and Seven Hills Trail to the edge of Ramapo Torne to enjoy more southerly views.

To complete the loop, turn east here and descend into a valley. The next rise brings you to a fire-scarred knoll. A level stretch ends in a scramble below Russian Bear, a freestanding rock outcrop beneath the cliff that the trail circles. As the trail curves back left on top of the cliff, you reach a vantage to the southwest with a pretty view to the ridge you were on about a half hour earlier.

The white-marked trail continues along the broad ridge through taller oaks on high ground, reaching an intersection after a forty-minute, mile walk from the intersection on the shoulder of Ramapo Torne. The circuit route calls for a right turn here, but you might want to explore a portion of the interconnecting trails you have missed. If so, turn left for a detour on the red-on-white-marked trail. It leads you down into a deep valley, then up a short rise, and down another steep ledge, to yet another intersection below Pulpit Rock. From here you can bushwhack up the ridge to your right (views possible only when leaves are off the trees) and walk back to your right along the top until you meet the trail again. This detour takes at least forty-five minutes.

Turning east from the four-way intersection, you are again walking through an area that has been ravaged by fire, which has created strange, yet beautiful compositions of trees and stumps. You will cross a jeep road that leads right into a steep glade. On a rise beyond, you intersect another old roadway, which the trail follows briefly to the southeast through a lovely laurel glade. At the next intersection, less than half a mile, but nearly half an hour distant, you meet the Kakiat Trail at an acute angle. Kakiat is the contraction of an Indian name for the

patent granted by the Governor of the Province of New York in 1696. The patent encompassed much of northern New Jersey and southern New York.

A left turn onto the Kakiat Trail would take you in 0.2 mile to a second intersection. The loop described here is a long 0.9 mile circuit over the Raccoon Brook Hills to the same intersection. The circuit is fun, so find the continuing route by walking southeast of the acute angle intersection on the Kakiat Trail for a hundred yards to find the Raccoon Hills Trail, which heads left into another valley,

Fire has created a weird landscape along parts of the trail in southern Harriman Park

this one with a swamp above that drains into a small stream that you will cross. The trail winds up ledges from the boulder-filled valley to an outcrop with views east to a desolate valley and north to Pine Meadow Lake. As you continue across the height of land, just before you begin to descend, you will find an opening with views to the west. There is a very steep descent into the next valley. It seems impossible, but this valley is even more choked with glacial boulders and erractics than the previous one.

From this valley it is only a short detour (with no real path) to Pine Meadow Lake, which you may want to visit. Return and follow the trail. As you go out of the valley, you will probably marvel at the number of ridges the trail designers have found for you to climb on this trip. A steep pitch down follows the next height of land, and it leads into a valley with a marvelous circle of erratics, a veritable Stonehenge built by the glacier. You meet a small stream coming in from your left—you will follow it as it grows and joins with others all the way back to your car. A hemlock grove shelters a campsite, and beyond you cross another stream, which tips sharply off to your right. Across the stream, and a bit uphill, you meet the Kakiat Trail, only to marvel at the hour it probably took you for the 0.9 mile loop and diversion. Now you leave the Raccoon Brook Hills Trail, turning right onto the Kakiat.

That trail begins to descend in earnest, following the stream that is on your right. Rock and laurel give way to pine and hemlock and even bigger boulders. Quickly you meet the Seven Bridges Trail as your trail comes to Pine Meadow Brook, enlarged by the addition of a tributary from the north. Stay on the south side of the brook, following the red-marked Pine Meadow Trail. It leads you fairly close to the stream with views of tremendous ledges above and to your left. When you cross the white-marked HTS trail again, which would lead you north on a bridge over the brook, you might want to stay close to the south side, bushwhacking along the stream for pictures of the waterfall that follows. This Cascade of Slid was named by Frank Place, one of the men who developed many of the trails within the park and contributed to the original edition of the *New York Walk Book*. Every hiker in Harriman State Park should read the *Walk Book* for its history of the men who built the trails and gave them their curious names. That reading will help you understand the peculiar development of the various trails and segments.

A path follows the north shore here, past the Cascade of Slid, but the south shore may be more interesting to the photographer. The red-marked trail also follows the brook, but well south of it, away from any views. At the second bridge, below the falls, you are near the confluence of Stony Brook and Pine Meadow Brook. Your route west continues on a well-walked but unmarked path beside the stream through a gorge that has everything it should, hemlock, rushing water, lovely vistas, and often the crowds who walk just far enough to appreciate the beauties of Stony Brook.

The next intersection will be with the red-marked trail, which comes in from the left. Beyond that point you will want to stop to appreciate the overhanging boulder above the stream. The trail is so easy walking that you should reach your car after following Pine Meadow Brook for about an hour. The ease of this stretch of the trail should take the kinks out of your legs, kinks that are obvious when you realize that it probably takes more than six hours for the rough six and a half miles you cover traversing the numerous steep hills that form the southern border of the park.

The Iron Mine Walk—Harriman State Park

Distance: 6.5 miles
Time: 5 hours
Vertical rise: 1,050 feet
Maps: USGS 7½′ Monroe; USGS 7½′ Popolopen Lake;
USGS 7½′ Thiells; USGS 7½′ Sloatsburg; NY–NJTC
Harriman–Bear Mtn., #4

Harriman State Park is full of historical walks, and the one that touches on a few of the region's nineteenth century iron mines blends good hiking with the annals of that time. Iron mining in the Ramapos actually dates back to 1742, although the Colonies had been an exporter of iron ore since 1718 and at the onset of the Revolutionary War were producing 14 percent of the world's iron. The iron ore of the Ramapo Hills, the nearby water-courses to power the bellows for the furnaces, the heavily wooded slopes whose timber yielded the necessary charcoal— all attracted entrepreneurs. The furnaces at Stirling, near Monroe, at Greenwood near the Ramapo, the Queensboro Fur-nace, and the Forest of Dean Furnace all produced iron for guns for the Revolu-tionary and Civil Wars. Mines were scat-tered through the Ramapo hills, furnaces were built, and settlements grew up around the furnaces.

The mines varied in depth from 10 to 6,000 feet, the deepest being the Forest of Dean Mine on the United States Mili-tary Reservation property. That mine's en-trance has been sealed. Many of the mines are water-filled and dangerous. This walk takes you past a few of the mines that can be inspected safely from the trail.

The mines you will walk past are in the Greenwood group, suppliers of the Greenwood furnace at Arden. This and other furnaces are described in *Vanishing Ironworks of the Ramapos* by James M. Ransom, a book to read if you wish to delve deeply into the history of the area. The Greenwood furnace was established about 1810 and supplied cannonballs to the American forces during the War of 1812. Robert Parrot acquired an interest in the furnace and surrounding lands in 1837, and he and his brother Peter managed the ironworks and became sole owners of it. With coal brought by the newly built railroad through the Ramapo Valley, the furnace's output increased until yearly production reached 5,000 tons of pig iron destined for fine hard-ware and stoves. During the Civil War, the iron was used for the famous Parrot gun, the most effective artillery weapon of the Union Army. This gun was made at the West Point foundry at Cold Spring under the direction of Robert Parrot. The

Beside the trail, a hemlock sits on a boulder like a brontosaurus on its egg

Echo Mtn

Echo Mtn

Island Pond Mtn
1303 x

Lemon Squeezer

TRAIL

PARK

nd
ad

APPALACHIAN

Surebridge Mountain

Surebridge Mountain

Surebridge Mountain

NATIONAL

Surebridge Swamp

367 x

RAMAPO-DUNDERBERG

SCENIC

TRAIL

Lost Mine Road

T U X E D

1300

1200

N

RAMAPO-DUNDERBERG

Times Square

Ship Rock
1353

Hogencamp Mountain

RAMAPO-DUNDERBURG

TRAIL

1300

Hogencamp Mtn

Pine Swamp

Pine Swamp Mtn

Lake Askoti

1200

Hogen Camp Mine

x 1096

T U X E D O

Lake Skannatati

P

ORANGE CO

ROCKLAND CO

1200

Camp

834

Little Long Pond

Camp
Little Long Pond

Lake

Kanawauke

Kanawauke Circle

829

DRIVE

Spring Pond

0   0.5   1.0 mile

PETES

, N.Y. 12464

moving of tables from sites, changing of sites unless office is notified. No more than 1 tent or 1 car on a site, no visitors, unless they register and pay. No objectional behavior. Place all trash in plastic bag ●IN DUMPSTER●.
Parents! Children are your responsibility. Swimming, tubing, boating are at your own risk. Do not remove any wood from piles until it is paid for. Check out time is 3 p.m. A fee is charges for early arrival or late departure. Disregarding any of the rules will be cause for asking you to leave, and no money will be refunded. We hope your stay will be pleasant and we thank you for visiting with us. Please come again.

Uncle Pete and Aunt Julie

914-688-5000

D1

UNCL

PHOENIC

RULES AND REGULATIONS

Welcome to our campground and our home. We cordially invite you and your family to Uncle Pete's. By law and understanding, we CANNOT permit any pets. We CANNOT permit vehicle traffic over 5 miles per hour, mini bikes, trail bikes, all terrain-vehicles, discharging of firearms or weapons, cutting or removing trees, plants or flowers, fishing without a license by anyone over 16 , fires, except in fireplaces provided, moving or enlarging fireplaces. No wood in fireplaces over 18" in length or 3" round. Quiet hours are from 10 p.m. to 8 a.m. Disposal of dishwater or sewage on ground is not permitted. No personal or dishwashing at water outlets, dishwashing in toilet sinks, small children in toilets unless accompanied, ore supplied by the Greenwood, Sure-bridge, Pine Swamp, O'Neil, and Clove mines was hauled to a kiln about a half mile above the furnace, where the ore was roasted to drive off sulfur, stamped to reduce it to the size of a "pigeon's egg," and then smelted in the furnace, which was built in the charming glen beside the outlet of Echo Lake.

To start the mine walk, find Seven Lakes Drive, which winds through the park from just north of Sloatsburg to the Long Mountain Parkway (NY 6) on the park's northern edge. Drive south from the Tiorati Circle on Seven Lakes Drive and turn right, opposite Lake Askoti, to a parking area for boating on Lake Skannatati. Two trails begin in the northwest corner of this lot, one marked with three red dots on a white blaze and the other with the turquoise-blue rectangle of the Long Path. Take the latter, which begins along the lake shore, leaving it near a northwest bay, to make a hop-a-rock crossing of an intermittent stream about twenty minutes from the trailhead.

A gentle uphill takes you to a gorgeous rock ledge; the route is through an open parklike area of tremendous oaks with laurel and blueberries beneath. Over a second ridge, a half hour from the start, you reach an abandoned roadway. Turn left here, where the way is marked with the yellow of the Dunning Trail as well as the turquoise-blue, and within a hundred yards turn right, away from the road, angling along the rocky hillside. The next half hour of walking takes you over that hill, across ridges, contouring the hillside beside a lovely hemlock-forested gorge, with balancing rocks along the trail, to a second road intersection. Here you turn left, joining the Arden-Surebridge Trail (the ASB—marked white with red as well as with the blue of the Long Path), and quickly reach (200 yards) the large erratic that marks Times Square, the intersection of the blue Long Path you have

been following with the red-marked Ramapo-Dunderberg Trail. You want to turn left on the red trail, toward Tuxedo.

On this portion of the route, you pass wonderful rock ledges, climb again over bare rocks with glacial striations, and enjoy views, mostly south over lovely rolling terrain falling away from Hogencamp Mountain at 1,353 feet. From the broad summit, the trail zigzags down across a ridge with signs of glaciers everywhere. In ten minutes you reach Ship Rock, a bottom-up prow of a boat. Just beyond it, make a sharp right turn. There are views all along as you cross an open rock ledge, conscious always of glacial activity from the telltale erratics and the striations and polishes on the ledges. Shortly you make another right turn, this time onto the Lichen Trail marked with a blue L on a white blaze. This picturesque section features tall laurel, ledges, and hemlock with occasional openings with views. The half-mile Lichen Trail drops sharply through an evergreen covered hillside to join the Arden-Surebridge Trail. At the crossing, turn left to follow again the blue squares of the Long Path, which leads you past a swamp and down a very pretty hemlock-covered hillside with a stream. As the trail levels out at the bottom of the hill, it makes a sharp right turn to pass a wet area and reach another intersection, this time with the white-marked Appalachian Trail. The blue trail turns right, and you take a middle route on the white-with-red-marked ASB and the AT, which both head toward the Lemon Squeezer. Across a small stream you begin to climb the hillside past a cliff with handsome split-off rock formations. The tiny stream contrasts with the violent forces of water and ice that over the years have created this scene with its impressive overhangs. Such a variety of impressions in only two hours of walking!

Where the rerouted AT with its white marks forks left, you turn right to begin the scramble into the Lemon Squeezer, although you could circle just left of it to avoid its craggy formation. After you squeeze between sheer rock walls and pull yourself over ledges through the gorge, markings for the AT and the ASB are obvious again. Follow the white-with-red blazes to the peak of Island Pond Mountain, an area more accessible from Tiorati or Arden Road. Off the trail to the right there are views of the valley between you and Surebridge Mountain. Just beyond, you reach a major trail intersection near an old foundation. Here you turn right on the AT and descend into a valley to cross a cleft and climb again to another ridge with limited views.

The following downhill leads to a left turn into a valley beside a dry streambed and along it for a five-minute walk to a right turn up through a draw. Near the top of the draw, a hemlock perches on a rock like a Brontosaurus on a giant egg. Beyond, the trail may be hard to follow as you continue climbing through the rocky draw. Just about three hours into the hike, you cross a hill beyond the draw, through a broadly open forest. A short descent through another small draw brings you to an abandoned roadway, below the ledges that define the eastern side of this small valley. From this intersection with the Lost Mine Road, you can see the tailings pit of the Greenwood Mine. Walk briefly left (north) along the road to examine its pit, which produced ore between 1838 and 1880 from three veins, the center one of which was nine feet thick.

Then, turn south on Lost Mine Road for one of the more charming parts of the walk. The roadway passes a handsome swamp and, if you know what to look for, signs of mining abound, tailing piles are everywhere and a few pits of the Surebridge Mine lie to the east of the road. As the road forks right, a causeway built up of tailings heads across a stream and the wet area of Surebridge Swamp. An arch of rhododendron shades the causeway, from which there are glimpses of the twisted stumps and wildflowers in the sphagnum bog.

A small rise leads to an intersection just short of Times Square. A brief detour north on the Ramapo–Dunderberg Trail (red dot) takes you to a half-round glacial pothole dripping with moss. Beyond Times Square, the red-triangle-marked ASB trail follows another old mining road, which you could follow until it intersects the Long Path. On this route you pass charcoal pits and more mine areas. The roadway turns south marked as the Dunning Trail (yellow). For one more mountaintop view, stay on the red-marked ASB. You pass another mine hole near the intersection. Then the ASB red trail turns away from the roadway to follow a narrower path, still marked with red, to wind up Pine Swamp Mountain. This twenty-minute climb offers an overlook across the lakes where the walk began, and a steep fifteen-minute descent brings you down to the trailhead.

Dunderberg Mountain and the Timp

Distance: 5 miles
Time: 5 hours
Vertical rise: 1,200 feet
Maps: USGS 7½' Popolopen Lake; USGS 7½' Peekskill;
  NY–NJTC Harriman–Bear Mtn., #4

The eastern end of the Dunderberg massif pinches the Hudson River to create the entrance to the narrows, at the southern end of the Hudson Highlands. Its western end is sharply defined by the cliff-faced Timp. The mountain stretches three miles in an almost east-west direction to form the northern border of Haverstraw Bay. This ponderous hulk inspired Washington Irving in *The Storm Ship* to tell of the Dutch goblin who "keeps the Donderberg" (sic) with speaking trumpet. Sailors reported hearing him in "stormy weather . . . giving orders in Low Dutch, for the piping up of a fresh gust of wind or the rattling off of another thunderclap." The hiker will find that the walk across Dunderberg's summit ridge to the Timp and back is one of the favorites in Bear Mountain, especially if your trip is planned to avoid the goblin's storms and give clear weather for the views.

If you can arrange two cars, a circuit offers even greater variety. Leave one car on the side of NY 9W near the entrance to the bird sanctuary on Iona Island, south of Bear Mountain State Park. Then drive south 2.2 miles to a small parking turnout on the east side of the road, just south of the high point of 9W's crossing of the Dunderberg shoulder.

You would never guess from the views here that such a marvelous sequence of lively vistas awaits you. The turnout overlooks Westchester County's new garbage-generated power plant and Indian Point's three nuclear power plants, scenes shielded from sight at all Dunderberg's vistas.

Across from the turnout by a rock cut, a red square on a white marker points you to the Ramapo-Dunderberg Trail. A short, steep climb brings you in fifteen minutes to the first view spot. This one looks north and east toward Peekskill with Bear Mountain visible through the trees. To the south, the Tappan Zee Bridge, High Tor, and Croton Point delineate the Hudson's course. Ten minutes later, more views open up as the trail parallels the deep cut that is the extension of Iona Bay. Black stumps punctuate the fire-ravaged hillside, and many trees are down. As you continue to climb, a detour to your left leads to another promontory with its higher perspective, and shortly another summit that seems equal in height to all the surrounding hills. Dunderberg, like Bear Mountain and Storm King to the north is topped with the igneous rocks of the last major magma invasion in the Hudson Highlands, an event that occurred between six and seven hundred million years ago.

You continue across the southern flank of the Dunderberg massif with glimpses through the trees downriver. Here and at several points along the trail you cross the graded and built-up bed of the old Dunderberg Railroad. Watch for its loops and switchbacks. This failed adventure was conceived in the late 1880s, when portions of it were built. It was planned to have a scenic, ten-mile gradual descent, looping around the mountain.

Your route is generally westerly, so that the next view spot overlooks Stony Point, with the Hook on the west and Croton,

Verplanck, and Indian Points on the east side of the river. The trail now crosses to Dunderberg's north side with limited views. A steep downgrade leads to a small pond in a cleft in the mountain and up another ledge with a view to the next ridge.

About an hour into the walk, northwest of the pond, you cross an obvious railroad bed. Beyond, a small opening overlooks the Hudson, while a second cut yields a glimpse of Taurus, Beacon, and Storm King. You continue across the broad hilltop with its small pond and out to another glimpse of Bear Mountain to the north. Beyond you see the summit of Bald Mountain, but to reach it you descend another draw. The trail has followed a variety of ledges, dark-stained and moss grown. At 2.3 miles you reach an intersection with a blue-marked Cornell Trail, which would take you down to Iona Bay. Woods roads create a five-way intersection here, and a section of the railroad is clearly obvious. You continue on just a few minutes more, less than 0.2 mile, to Bald Summit with the deep pit of the Cornell Mine to the north of the summit.

If the winds are northwesterly, you may want to wait to picnic, for the very next vantage point, less than 0.4 mile south, is a sheltered southern one with the skyline of New York City on the horizon. Beyond the trail heads sharply down, briefly beside a stream, then across the stream toward the hill that lies east of the Timp. Beyond the stream, Timp Brook, which veers to the right, the trail is crowded with laurel. Gemlike scenes, views back to Bald, moss on the path, a small valley, all lead up to a roadway that was the route of the 1777 British march to capture Fort Montgomery. Cross it and continue toward the Timp, which you reach shortly, completing about a leisurely three hour, 3.5-mile walk. Here, the day's best views toward the city skyline or north past Bear Mountain Bridge reward you.

The continuing trail drops down to the south, barely skirting the cliffs on the Timp's southwestern face on a rock-strewn route. The sharp drop is first to

Cliffs of the Timp

the east, then a zigzag back west across the face of the cliff. Needless to say, this is a place for caution. The blue-marked Timp-Torne trail from Tomkins Cove comes in from the left, and beyond it you could begin the climb of one more ridge on either a red or blue trail to make a bigger loop walk. But, perhaps it is time to head down, and a red-marked ski trail turning right starts you in that direction, along the route of Timp Pass Road. From it, there is a lovely view of the uplifted layers of rock that form the Timp. You have left the realm of scrubby oaks and windswept summit ridges and returned to taller forests as you follow the roadway down. Its washed-out condition can make rough walking. A stream from a hill to the east begins to follow the roadway, and overhanging ledges close in.

At a T intersection, 0.8 mile from the Timp, your route meets a road from the Cornell Mine and Bald Mountain, which has roughly paralleled Timp Brook. This route is also a part of the 1777 march route. Here you turn left and cross the brook near some stone foundations and a lean-to. The road is now level and easy to walk, quickly leading you through abandoned farmlands marked by old apple trees. From a field with front porch maples you have a glimpse of the Bald Mountain summit. After you recross the brook, watch for the arrow that indicates a ski trail crossing. Take this route to the right, around a huge glacial erratic, and down to cross the brook once more. The trail leads up a small hill past a swamp over which you can look back to Dunderberg. The route is basically north and down to the Doodletown Reservoir. Just before you reach the reservoir, you will see a blue trail that forks right to follow a ledge above the deep ravine of the reservoir's outlet. This handsome segment of trail exits on 9W near the entrance to Iona Bird Sanctuary, a delightful place to extend your outing. The sanctuary is on an island once known as Weyant's Island after its first owner, now as Iona Island after Dr. C. W. Grant, who inherited it from his father-in-law in the 1850s. He farmed choice fruits here, maintained a vineyard, and give it its curious name when he claimed "I-own-an-island."

Popolopen Gorge and The Torne

Distance: 8 miles
Time: 5½ hours
Vertical rise: 700 feet
Maps: USGS 7½' Popolopen Lake; USGS 7½' Peekskill;
   NY–NJTC Harriman–Bear Mtn., #4

Popolopen Torne has one of the Hudson Highland's most surprising views. Popolopen Gorge, early in spring with high water and fewer visitors, is one of Bear Mountain State Park's most charming spots. Put them together and you have a splendid walk.

Park, for a $2.50 fee, in the lot off NY 9W near the Bear Mountain Inn, and walk north along the shores of Hessian Lake and out to NY 9. Walk cautiously along the highway to the traffic circle, and cross both lanes of the Bear Mountain Parkway. Walk on the grass along the triangle that separates the parkway from the NY 9 access road, and cross that roadway. Directly opposite, a road closed to traffic by a gate leads north. Take it to the intersection with another roadway from NY 9, where unfortunately there is no parking. Follow this roadway left, west, guided by red markers that lead you to a trail beside the Hell Hole on the Popolopen Gorge.

East of here, Popolopen Brook flows between two "rocky promontories on which stood Forts Clinton (south) and Montgomery (north), within rifle-shot of each other. The banks of the creek are high and precipitous, the southern one

covered with trees; and less than half a mile from its broad and deep mouth in which large vessels may anchor, it is a wild mountain stream—rushing into the placid tyde-water through narrow valleys and dark ravines." Here at the foot of wild cascades, Benson J. Lossing, chronicler of the Hudson, sat in the 1850s to sketch the scene. "A short dam has been constructed there for sending water through a flume to a mill a few rods below. This stream . . . presents a thousand charming pictures, where nature woos her lovers in the pleasant summer-time." The forts disappeared long ago, but Lossing's description is still appropriate.

The forts played a pivotal role during the Revolution. They were constructed at the beginning of the Revolutionary War, and a chain was strung between Fort Montgomery and Anthony's Nose across the Hudson to stop British ships that tried to reach West Point. In October 1777, under the command of Sir Henry Clinton, the British attacked making an arduous trip over Dunderberg. A skirmish at Hessian Lake led to its nickname as "Bloody Pond;" the forts were overcome, with the Americans suffering 300 casualties to

150 for the British. American ships, two frigates, two galleys, and an armed sloop tried to escape upriver, but, without wind, they were abandoned by their crews who set them afire to prevent the British from capturing them.

Your walk along Popolopen Brook is west away from the site of the forts. The Hell Hole, a pool below a triple waterfall with deep pools and cascades below, greets you as you reach Popolopen Creek, a delightful place to photograph. Beyond the Hell Hole, the trail continues its western course, climbing behind the dam that holds back a lovely hemlock-shrouded pond. The western edge of the pond is punctuated by a small waterfall, upstream from which the gorge narrows and deepens. The trail will continue west following the course of the creek, interrupted by trail intersections, old roadways, and informal paths to the pools and rapids along the stream's course, which is best seen in high water. Sharp, moss-covered rocks, dark hemlocks, and white-barked sycamores frame the frolicking stream. The crash of water drowns out all road sounds, for the highway is not that far away. You pass a fork to the

Popolopen Brook in spring

right, not clearly marked, but in sight of a bridge over the stream. You will return here later, so mark the spot. The Torne is clearly visible here, to the north above the gorge.

Within an hour and a quarter, even if you dawdle, you will find the trail swings left, uphill, away from the gorge. You may want to bushwhack farther along the stream, although the steep ledges often make the going rough. The stream levels out beyond a small dam, and soon you meet another trail marked with several blazes: a blue dot on a white square, the red of the Timp-Torne Trail, and a diamond with a blue 79, denoting this as part of the route the Americans followed in 1779 when they attempted to retake control of the Hudson River. Follow these trails as they continue along the now quiet watercourse. Within sight of the parkway, you cross a promontory to a bridge over the stream which now has been forced into a narrow sluiceway. Here the trail meets a roadway. The way right leads to West Point lands and the

Queensboro Furnace, but this area is not open to the public. The trail follows the roadway left toward Queensboro Lake, but you will follow it only briefly before making a right turn from it to continue on the red-marked Popolopen Gorge Trail. This leads across the north edge of Queensboro Lake and on to Turkey Hill Lake. At Queensboro Lake you will find a choice picnic spot on a laurel-covered promontory overlooking the water. To reach the spot, turn off the trail, within sight of the lake and head right, north, for 200 yards.

For the return walk, stay on the trail with its blue and red markers. It takes the high road nearer the rim of the gorge. When the trail turns to descend into the gorge, begin to look closely for the fork to turn left toward Popolopen Brook. You cross the brook and begin to climb up to an abandoned roadway, following it briefly to climb again to cross an aqueduct and finally to reach Mine Road. The trail continues across the road, leading up the Torne. There are views almost from the beginning along this short scramble. Bear Mountain blocks all views south, but

Anthony's Nose is prominent to the east beyond this narrowest bend in the river. A twenty-minute climb from the roadway brings you to the summit. On the open rock of the Torne you will find both white and turquoise blazes. These mark a trail leading north for a view over West Point lands to an easier descent, which is less steep after the first ledge.

On the return to the roadway, watch for where an old dirt road forks toward the gorge. Here, you can easily climb down to follow the aqueduct east toward Fort Montgomery. This side of the gorge is so steep you will not be tempted to leave the aqueduct route to walk closer to water level. The aqueduct trail emerges near the intersection of Mine Road and Cedar Drive. You will follow Mine Road for a quarter mile until a sign on a lightpost directs you back onto a hemlock-shaded road on Park land again. At a fork on this roadway, a right choice would lead you steeply down into the gorge near the Hell Hole. The way left leads up to another roadway within sight of NY 9W. Walk carefully along the shoulder of 9W back to your car.

**Central
Hudson
Highlands**

View of Storm King from Taurus

Taurus

Distance: 6 miles
Time: 4 hours
Vertical rise: 1,400 feet
Map: USGS 7½′ West Point; NY–NJTC East Hudson
    Trails, #11

The loop on Taurus has been a favorite with hikers for many years, but recent changes in the pattern of land ownership have forced the New York–New Jersey Trail Conference to reroute a portion of it. The resulting loop possibilities actually are improved, except that now there is no single trailhead possible. The best solution seems to be a loop walk with a short return segment along a highway and through the charming town of Cold Spring. This way the best of the traditional route is preserved, and a very handsome new segment directly opposite Crow's Nest is added. Both ends of the trail have been poorly marked in recent years, but new marking should be in place now.

Cedar Street is a north turn from NY 301, 0.3 mile east of NY 9D. A short block later, Mountain Street is a left turn. Park along the street here, not in the American Legion Parking lot. If parking on the narrow streets is a problem, you can park on 9D, a mile north of 301, at the trailhead for the northern segment of this loop, which may be concealed in the brush on the right side of the road. You can walk through the charming village to this southern trailhead—a walk short enough that two cars are really not necessary.

Opposite Mountain Street, three turquoise marks on a utility pole indicate the Three Notch Trail, which begins by following an old road. You will discover several intersections with other woods roads, all of which have been extensively used by all-terrain vehicles. The route north-northwest is obvious if marking is kept up. Otherwise, you may follow a few false starts. A compass here to keep you on course will help. Your route is level, heading north beneath stately trees along the mountain's base, with half dozen forks enroute. After you have walked for twenty minutes, you find the trail crossing a paved road at right angles. From here on the way is the most direct. Shortly beyond, at 1 mile, you cross the Catskill Aqueduct, which emerges from deep within Taurus. Now you begin a lovely woodland walk.

The deep woods charm of the historical roadway approach to Taurus's summit always appeals. The handsome rockwork base that holds the traverse dates to a nineteenth-century attempt to put a hotel on Taurus's summit.

Less than thirty minutes beyond the macadam road crossing, the roadway levels out. Watch for the intersection at

2.3 miles where the turquoise trail forks right, the roadway goes straight ahead, and the white-marked Washburn Trail is a left fork. You may follow the white trail straight toward the summit, or you can follow the roadway leisurely as it zigzags up, twice crossing the white trail. Your first view from the trail, not fifty feet from the second road crossing, is to the northeast. Just beyond, the trail follows the road to an overlook north toward Beacon, with the jagged outline of Breakneck Ridge leading down to the Hudson opposite the point where the Storm King massif rises.

A five-minute walk beyond leads to an unmarked path that angles left as the roadway bends right. That path leads in a hundred feet to a southern overlook, often the most protected picnic spot on Taurus's summit. You see Constitution Island with West Point across the river, framing the southern narrows of the Hudson Highlands. Above the highlands, you see the distant skyline of New York City. Just north of Constitution Island on the banks of Foundry Brook stood the famous West Point Foundry, referred to in the Mines walk of Harriman Park and the walk through Fahnestock. The foundry was incorporated by an act of the New York State legislature in 1818. From mines in the nearby hills, the foundry produced more than 3,000 cannons, which could shoot up to 400-pounders, and over 1,600,000 projectiles. Buildings from the foundry remain in Cold Spring, but they are not open to the public. However, the Foundry Museum of the Putnam County Historical Society, just south of NY 301 off NY 9, has a fascinating collection of local history (open all day Wednesday and Saturday afternoon).

Returning to and continuing on the roadway, you pass the summit and then, following a narrow, steep footpath, head downhill. Here a chain of fabulous views commences, first with an overlook north to Storm King and Breakneck and south to Bear Mountain and Dunderberg. Angling right and down you pause at an overlook opposite Storm King. Imagine the days when the foundry was producing the Parrot guns and testing the cylinders of those rifled cannons with their unique coiled construction by loading them to full capacity and aiming them at the rocky front of Storm King across the river. The bursting shells threw up enormous masses of earth, and the impressions were visible for years. Strange are the origins of the scars that now make up the Hudson River scenery.

From this vantage on fine views are almost continuous. At one spot you seem to be suspended directly over the Hudson. Forty minutes from the summit, you will have dropped down to the level of taller trees, and the views disappear. Here, a sign tells you of the closed section of trail that used to lead back to the trailhead where you began. The new route is full of surprises.

The trail leads out across a shoulder of the mountain to a view spot precipitously perched above the Hudson facing Crow's Nest. Then, the steep and often rubble-strewn route takes you out to the top of a quarry where you intersect an abandoned road on its southern flank. The quarry, where work began in the 1930s, produced an ugly scar that precipitated the drive to have the State acquire this land, eventually forming around it and the mountains to the north the Hudson Highlands State Park.

Following the road around the south side of the quarry to a field below it, the marked trail then takes a right fork through the field, away from the road. One more steep section brings you out to another relocation marker, and just beyond to the trailhead on NY 9D. Turn left up the highway to NY 301 and then east, left, to your car. The walk along the roads, just over a mile, adds less than half an hour to the one-and-a-half-hour descent from the summit.

7

Breakneck Ridge and Sugarloaf Mountain

Distance: 5.5 miles
Time: 4 to 4½ hours
Vertical rise: 1,450 feet
Map: USGS 7½' West Point; NY–NJTC East Hudson
   Trails, #11

"Eastward a high chain of mountains whose sides were covered with woods up to no more than half of their height. The summits, however, were quite barren; for I suppose nothing would grow there on account of the great degree of heat, dryness, and the violence of the wind to which that part was exposed." Thus, the Swedish botanist, Peter Kalm, observed the Hudson Highlands on the east side of the river in 1749. One highlight of his trip was his discovery and the first botanical description of the American mountain laurel, *Kalmia latifolia,* the shrub that grows on every slope from the Ramapos to the Shawangunks and whose blooms make walking here and everywhere in southern New York in late May and early June so special.

For a time, Breakneck was known as Turk's Face. According to the British traveler, John Maude, writing in 1800, "the profile of the Face Mountain so strongly resembles the profile of the human face, that I had for some time my doubts whether art had not assisted in improving the likeness. I have seen other blockheads which did not possess so sensible a countenance." According to Benson Lossing, a blast from a quarry on the side of the mountain dislodged

the head, complete with a "thick curly beard upon the chin," making it look like a Turk. Sometime after the head disappeared, a runaway bull was rumored to have climbed the mountain and fallen to its death when pursued, giving rise to the name Breakneck. In the first few hundred feet of scrambling up Breakneck's serrated face, you may wonder if the name refers to crazy hikers.

Judging by the cars that line NY 9D, two miles north of Cold Spring, near the underpass and trailhead below Breakneck Ridge's cliffs and jagged skyline, it is easy to believe that the mountain is everyone's favorite in the Hudson Highlands. On occasion you will find crowds on the region's steepest scramble, but the higher you go, the fewer climbers you will meet, and if you follow the described loop, you will enjoy not only the fabulous climb, but you also will get away to more remote and especially delightful vantages.

Park at the roadside just north of the underpass, and begin this loop walk on the west side of the road where you will find the white-blazed Breakneck Ridge Trail by climbing south along the road and over the overpass. The well-worn route is a wild scramble of nearly a thou-

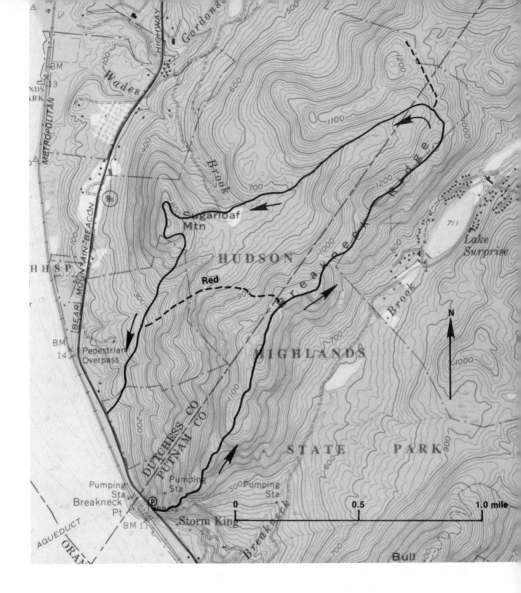

sand feet in a third of a mile, and comparable to a climb up the Empire State Building, with views at every level. Scramble to me means using your hands, and you will appreciate an old pair of gloves to protect them from the rough and most resistant of the highland rocks, the Precambrian magma intrusion that crests Breakneck Ridge.

In thirty minutes you will reach a first knob, the destination of most climbers. Your route is to the right along the cliff top. The trail has been designed to take advantage of the wildest scrambles, and you will note that below the first knob and twice on the way to the second, white arrows and a sign painted "alt." direct you to alternate easier routes.

The first mile and a half of the trip is a series of knobs, false summits on the way to the 1,200 foot crest. The second knob reveals a third as well as views north to the cone of Sugarloaf. You continue traversing the rock face just above the cliff with another knob looming above you. This third in the sequence is more deceptive than the rest, for, upon reaching it, you discover the trail dips into a small valley before rising to a fourth knob. This hawk's perch is followed by a deeper, wooded ravine, above which the fifth knob looms. Here you have a fine view to the northwest.

Another rise brings you to the west face of the fifth knob, overlooking Bannerman's Island, Sugarloaf, and the Newburgh–Beacon Bridge with the Shawangunks beyond and the Catskills outlining the distant horizon. It takes a pretty steady climb of an hour and a quarter to reach this point. Breakneck continues north as a narrow ridge with the trail winding from side to side to take advantage of the overlooks. And, its warty surface continues to offer a series of knobs to climb. A sixth distinct knob is open to the east with views of the heavily wooded Lake Surprise Valley. A walk along the thin ridge separates this vantage from the seventh knob where the trail first brings you to an overlook to the east and then across the height of land to a western vantage. A gentle descent and an equally short rise bring you to a well-marked fork where the red trail heads west toward Sugarloaf.

This red trail, reached at 1.5 miles after an hour and a half, would provide a shorter, alternate loop. It descends 0.6 mile, passing one good overlook, to join the last half mile of the yellow trail you will follow to complete the longer loop outlined. So, continue straight ahead. A small rise opens out to a view of the wooded and deceptively gentle eastern slope of Sugarloaf. Beyond, the trail dips into a deep valley that lies beneath the eighth knob. As you start steeply down

into the valley, a blue-marked trail from Surprise Valley comes in from the right, and blue markers continue with the white. Even the valley has its ups and downs, and a final rubble-filled draw precedes a steep climb to a spot on the knob that looks southwest to Black Rock Forest. A second vantage overlooks Lake Surprise. It takes about half an hour to reach this knob from the red trail intersection. As you start down its northern flank you view a wooded knob ahead. This one you will not climb, for you will look for an abandoned roadway in the valley between.

The trail continues on the east side of the ridge, descending into the less exposed region of taller trees. At 2.5 miles, fifteen minutes from the last summit, the trail, marked mostly with blue, intersects a roadway. The route right is unmarked, while the trail follows the road left for a hundred yards and forks right again along the ridge. At this point, stay on the unmarked road, which heads generally west-southwest. Don't be too mesmerized by the delights of this woodland road, for you will have to find and follow an unmarked path that leads left away from it. To discover this fork, mark the following clues. If you follow the road down for a ten-minute walk, you will discover an often waterless brook and a valley on your right. An equal distance beyond, at about 0.6 mile after leaving the red-marked trail, you will cross over the valley to follow the stream on its right bank. After walking along the right bank for three hundred yards, you should notice a left fork and a narrow trail heading steeply down to the stream. Take it, for the continuation of the road you have been following leads to private lands.

Across the stream another roadway leads up and to the left, passing a field

Storm King from Breakneck

across which lies Sugarloaf. About 200 yards beyond the stream, the woods road angles sharply right and downhill, following the course of the stream. At this point, a second, less distinct road goes straight ahead and quickly becomes a roadway choked to a narrow path with grasses and marked infrequently with yellow. Take this route to the western edge of the field beyond a chimney of a long-gone farmhouse and around to the woods beyond where you climb toward the south. A hundred yards up the slope, the yellow trail turns right, continuing uphill around the northern flank of the mountain. Along the way, you have through-the-trees views of Beacon before reaching an overlook with a broad expanse of the Hudson between you and the gradual western slopes that lead up to the high peaks of the Catskills. The 1.25 mile walk from the ridge north of Breakneck down the valley and up to Sugarloaf's first outlook should take less than an hour.

The yellow trail known as the Wilkinson Memorial Trail, winds south across Sugarloaf's summit to a second overlook, this one more southerly. The southeast face is a little less steep than the cone's western flanks, but the route the yellow-marked Wilkinson Memorial Trail takes you on is still quite precipitous. As the trail levels out beside a hemlock-filled valley, you turn left into that valley and up to a roadway. Here the trail turns right along the roadway and quickly reaches a giant oak with three red blazes, which indicates the western end of the red trail.

The yellow trail follows the roadway down for the most part, crossing a small ravine, and yielding but one view, a glimpse across a ravine toward the top of Storm King. The route is through a field, past a huge stone foundation, and finally out to the highway. The descent from Sugarloaf requires but twenty minutes for the 800-foot, nearly mile-long drop. You reach the highway, NY 9D, a quarter-mile north of the trailhead from which you started.

Storm King

Distance: 7 miles
Time: 5½ hours
Vertical rise: 1,200 feet
Maps: USGS 7½′ Cornwall; USGS 7½′ West Point

"The Montaynes look as if some Metall or Minerall were in them. For the trees that grow on them were all blasted, and some of them barren with few or no trees on them." Thus did Robert Juet describe his view of the Hudson Highlands in September 1609 from Henry Hudson's boat, anchored in what is now Newburgh Bay after his first trip up the Hudson. The centuries have done little to alter the view.

The noble ring of hills through which the Hudson flows south of Newburgh is as impressive as any range in the state. Storm King guards the west bank and Beacon giving way to Breakneck Ridge and Taurus on the south guards the eastern shores. They are all mountains you will climb again and again.

Storm King and Butter Hill form a semicircular crest that Benson Lossing believed the Dutch skippers thought of as a hugh lump of butter, hence the original name Boterberg. Nathaniel Parker Willis, who settled at Idlewild at the foot of Storm King in present day Cornwall, wrote weekly letters to the *Home Journal* in the 1850s describing his bucolic surroundings. It was he who was able to change part of the mountain's name to the more romantic Storm King.

There are several ways to savor the walk on Storm King and Butter Hill. Sometimes, the opportunity to get away for a short excursion makes the walk from NY 9W across the vantages just west of Storm King's summit seem like a perfect outing. This is a round trip walk of about three miles with a climb of 350 feet, for a three hour excursion. The walk can be extended by a descent toward Cornwall and a visit to the Museum of the Hudson Highlands, with distance, time, and elevation as noted above.

Take NY 9W as it climbs the hills north and west of West Point. There is a large parking turnout at the height of land on Butter Hill, just before the highway descends toward Cornwall. From the north of the turnout, and quite close to the highway, the Stillman Trail, with its trailhead unmarked, begins its ascent. Yellow blazes finally appear on the open rock crossings. The trail climbs the ridge near the road to a stone foundation, then winds into a stone-filled valley. A sharp right across the draw at the head of the valley heads up sharply to the first knob with a narrow view of the river.

Notice all along the signs of an old burn that swept this hilltop. Somehow, the laurel and much of the oak survive.

A gentle walk to the next knob on Butter Hill yields views of Cold Spring and the quarry north of it on the slopes of Taurus. A few minutes more walking bring you to the height of land on Butter Hill with its survey markers. This spot, only thirty minutes from the start, has views of the summit of Breakneck Ridge and Beacon.

Good views north and west accompany you as you walk north, especially when the leaves are down, permitting the range from Schunemunk to the Shawangunks to stand out in front of the distant blue hills of the Catskills. The walk on the northwestern flanks ends in a sharp right marked by yellow blazes as the trail reaches Storm King. The trail continues on the northern flanks of Storm King with occasional view spots opening up en route. Stunted pine frame the vistas: the broad sweep of river, punctuated by Bannerman's or Pollepel Island, that lies 1,300 feet below your perch. This mysterious island has a strange tale. Jasper Dankers, a minister, recorded in 1680 that it was called Potlepels Eylant, Dutch

for Potladle Island. General Clinton fortified it in 1777 along with Constitution Island to the south. In the 1850s, Lossing reported that it was home to a solitary house that looked like a wren's nest, inhabited by a fisherman with an insane wife who thought herself to be the Queen of England. Francis Bannerman bought the island to house his arsenal of secondhand military supplies, arms captured in the Spanish-American War. It was he who built the replica of a Scottish Castle whose remains you see. He had a thriving military supply business until the United States government made it illegal for citizens to sell arms to foreign governments.

The trail continues, gradually descending, to a final opening overlooking the river east and southeast. It is delightful to picnic here and retrace your steps, but time permitting, you can continue along the trail for the steep descent, a real scramble at first, to the west.

Storm King from Butter Hill

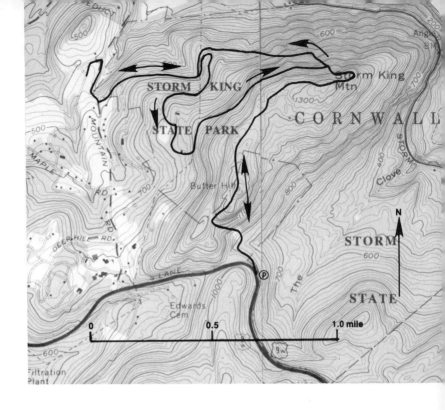

The trail drops 700 feet in a half a mile. About two-thirds of the way through the steepest drop, as the trail seems to level out, you will notice two unmarked paths coming in from your right. You may wish to experiment with one of them on your return. You continue the zigzag route of the yellow trail, coming out to a promontory with views up toward Beacon. A hundred feet further, the trail reaches and follows a dirt roadway out to Mountain Road. Here turn right, then left to reach the Museum of the Highlands, open Monday-Thursday and weekend afternoons. It houses a natural history collection highlighted by a collection of owls and snakes that live in these mountains, but which you rarely see. If you have opted for the longer trek, you can enjoy a picnic beside a stream at the rear of the museum.

On the return, stay on the abandoned roadway. It once led to a stone building constructed by Italian stone masons before World War I. The ruins lie at the end of the roadway that zigzags up the mountain. It must have been a handsome place, if the stonework along the road is any indication. Note the beautiful arch that carries the road over a small stream just before the Stillman Trail forks left. And notice too the huge grape vines curled around a nearby tree like a serpent in the Garden of Eden.

The road forks after a twenty-minute walk; the foundations lie to the left. Walking through them to a stone stairway in a wall at the far end, you will find the beginning of an unmarked path that contours around the slopes to intersect the Stillman Trail again. From here it is a stiff twenty-minute climb to the crest of Storm King, where you can retrace your steps to the parking turnout.

Black Rock Forest—Southern Ledges

Distance: 6.5 miles
Time: 5 hours
Vertical rise: 850 feet
Map: USGS 7½' Cornwall

The wonderful hiking trails in Black Rock Forest are among the region's least used. They wind around and over a dozen peaks with elevations over 1,400 feet. But these peaks rise generally less than 400 feet from the high plateau that is a westward continuation of the Storm King intrusion of the Hudson Highlands. That plateau drops precipitously to the west and north, with the dark summit of Black Rock Mountain, namesake of the forest, standing out above the valley near Cornwall.

In 1949, the 3,600-acre forest was given to Harvard University for research by Dr. Ernest Stillman, whose father had acquired the property over many years. Research in silviculture that has been done over the years is described in a series of Black Rock Forest Bulletins. The future of that research is uncertain however, for Harvard now wants to turn over the management of the forest to a New York State institution. A feature of any walk in the forest is the sight of distinctive plots of native trees, each with differing timber management techniques. All but one of the half-dozen ponds are parts of water systems for nearby towns, so laws prohibit use of them in any way. Dirt roads connect the different plots and are used by the forest's managers, but public

vehicular traffic is not permitted. The Black Rock Game Club has sole permission to hunt these lands for the numerous deer that populate the forest, so hiking during deer hunting season is prohibited. And, as in all the Hudson Highlands, fire is a problem, so there are prohibitions against fires in any form. It is expected that public access will continue even if the property changes hands.

There are two eastern entrances to Black Rock Forest from NY 9W and one from Mine Road on the west. This hike will start at an eastern trailhead and wind along the southern ledges that border on United States Military Academy posted lands. Both hikes described in this area will combine roads with marked trails to give a fair sample of the variety the forest has to offer.

Drive north on NY 9W past an entrance to West Point and over the shoulder of Storm King, and take the first right turn onto Mountain Road. Immediately turn right again, under the highway and onto a narrow road that leads to the Upper Reservoir where you can park. If you continue north on 9W for 0.7 mile beyond Mountain Road, a right turn brings you to the Park Headquarters where maps are available.

Walk west from the reservoir along the

0   0.5   1.0 mile

Black Rock Hollow

Filtration Plant

Edwards Cem

LANE

Whitehorse Mtn

Upper Reservoir

Filter House

Mt Misery

Black Rock

Aleck Meadow Reservoir

Hill of Pines

Sphagnum Pond

Arthurs Pond

Chatfield Road

Sutherland Pond

Tamarack Pond

Spy Rock

Bog Meadow Road

Rattlesnake Hill

Bog Meadow Pond

Lookout Tower

Jims Pond

Eagles Cliff

N

H I G H L A N D S

Highland

293

park road. In a quarter-mile, a five-minute walk, you will see yellow blazes on the left side of the road that denote the Stillman Trail, one of the two principal trails that traverse the forest. Follow this route up Misery Hill through laurel stands with trailing arbutus. The short twenty-minute climb seems steeper than its 300-foot rise above the reservoir, but it yields views of Black Rock Mountain and Aleck Meadow Reservoir. An equally steep descent follows, through rugged and rock-strewn terrain. "Storm King granite weathers in some areas into distinctive plates and in others into a rubbly pile of decayed rock."* The trail is composed of the latter. As the yellow trail levels out, it forks right, but you continue straight for a hundred feet or so to a second intersection. Here, at 0.6 mile, the blue Swamp Trail forks right, but you again go straight ahead, now on the white-marked Scenic Trail.

This trail begins another rough climb over a rock-strewn trail, up the Hill of Pines. You approach an opening with a view below the summit, where double white markers and a cairn direct you up and left to the summit with its view south-southwest over lakes and the fire tower summit. The white trail now leads down through a narrow rock cleft to an open knob with views all around. Notice how flat the summits of all the visible mountains seem, how equal their heights.

With a sharp right turn, the white trail leads down to a draw, then briefly up before the final descent to a dirt road, a mile from the start. Turn right on it and then immediately left, essentially crossing it to begin a climb again. You quickly attain a ridge, then drop sharply down about fifty feet to walk on a relatively

level high ledge near the southern boundary of the park. You can see one of the day's destinations, Spy Rock, ahead over ponds and lower hills. As you continue on the ledges past a sequence of lovely view spots, you look ahead to Eagle Cliff, also one of your destinations.

A steep descent follows, circling around and switchbacking down again near the park boundary. At 1.9 miles, a double white marker alerts you to a left turn along Bog Meadow Road. In a quarter-mile, a yellow trail forks right from your white-marked route toward Arthur's Pond and the fire tower, but you continue on the road, passing a pit privy at an intersection 2.5 miles and about two-and-a-quarter hours into the walk.

Just past the privy, jog right then left on the road, then back to walking on a white-marked trail. After five minutes of following this trail, begin to watch carefully for a cairn—it will alert you to an unmarked path on the right that leads 200 yards to a rock outcrop on Spy Rock. Here the Hudson Valley appears incongruously on your left as it bends into the Hudson Highlands. The view beyond the valley is toward the Gunks with the Catskills beyond. South Beacon and Breakneck Ridge define the horizon on your right. At 1,463 feet, this is the highest point in the western Hudson Highlands.

As you return to the ledge trail and continue quickly along it, watch carefully. In another five minutes, at about 200 yards, you should see three yellow blazes on a rock on the right side of the trail. Mark it well, for you will retrace your steps to this spot after a visit to Eagle Cliff. Next, on the white trail, you will see, on your left, a yellow trail to Jims Pond. Very shortly beyond, three blue markers direct you left to the knob of Eagle Cliff, 1,443 feet high, from which you can see the skyline of New York City beyond An-

---

*Christopher J. Schuberth, *The Geology of New York and Environs* (Garden City, NY: Natural History Press, 1968), p. 258.

View from the southern ledges of Black Rock Forest

thony's Nose, Bear Mountain, Dunderberg, and the Timp. It takes less than three hours to reach this spot, 3.6 miles from the beginning, which makes it ideal for a lunch break.

Return to the white Scenic Trail, and retrace your steps to the three yellow blazes on the rock. Here, a left turn puts you on a narrow path over a rise, past an old wooden fire tower. A gentle descent brings you in a quarter-mile to an intersection, where the yellow trail makes a sharp left turn. You should turn right on a blue trail, which leads in a hundred yards to Chatfield Road. Turn right on it past Tamarack Pond, which you partly circle.

The next milestone on the road, near the intersection of Tamarack and Continental Roads, just over a mile from Eagle Cliff, is a marvelous old stone building with a beehive oven. It is Chat-field House, built in 1834 as a farmhouse. It was gutted by fire in 1908 and restored in 1932 by Dr. Stillman. The lands nearby were once pastures and orchard. And, shallow Tamarack Pond, originally called Orchard Pond, was used as a cranberry bog.

Turn left on Continental Road to a point opposite the foot of Arthurs Pond, which is across the road from Chatfield House. The yellow trail takes you across the dam and its spillway where it turns right along the pond. You want a white trail that heads left, away from the pond, almost parallel to the spillway. This route takes you quickly down to a road beside Aleck Meadow Reservoir. Here, you could go right and back to the road and quickly end the trip, but instead turn left toward Black Rock Mountain. As you cross a stream, turn right on a yellow trail, which immediately splits. Take the right turn here, which leads you across the reservoir's dam. Turn left on the road below the dam, which takes you in 0.6 mile back to the parking area.

10

Black Rock Forest—Northern Loop

Distance: 5.5 miles
Time: 3½ hours
Vertical rise: 600 feet
Map: USGS 7½' Cornwall

There is a small trailhead for the trails in Black Rock Forest on the northwestern side of the forest that is ideal for this loop hike. To find it, drive north on NY 9W to Angola Road, near Central Valley. Head southwest on Angola Road for 1.6 miles, then turn left on Mine Hill Road and go 0.9 mile to the turnout. The Rich Mine in this vicinity was described in 1837 by Lewis C. Beck, a professor of chemistry at Rutgers. It was a part of the Monroe Iron Works, owned by Hudson McFarlan, which produced quantities of nails and hoop iron dating back to 1808.

The trail begins opposite the uphill end of the turnout and is marked by three yellow diamonds. The faint beginning leads sharply uphill on a traverse that immediately offers views of Schunemunk and the Catskills. The trail is carefully marked, with double diamonds indicating switchbacks.

After a ten-minute climb, a triple marker alerts you to an intersection; the yellow diamond trail that forks right will be your return route. Take the left fork, marked with yellow circles to a series of overlooks on open rock ledges. You continue on the ridge on high ground at the border of deeper forests, then descend slightly into them. Cross a small stream

by hopping rocks, and walk through a wet area with trout lilies and violets. Beyond, a small rise leads to an old road, a mile from the start, but just before you reach it, the yellow trail makes a sharp left. It is easy to miss the turn, but if you do, a left turn on the road will do, for the yellow trail reaches the road again in less than 200 yards. At this point, a sharp right on a blue trail could take you over Sacketts Mountain. You will continue on the roadway, which bears yellow markers for 75 yards to a point where the road angles left and the yellow trail takes off right, uphill.

You follow the trail as it traverses the mountain through a tall oak stand, glimpsing the roadway below and left. Your route parallels the road somewhat, then climbs, crosses a bridge near a spring, and rejoins the road, which you follow for 200 feet to a road barrier. Continental and Sutherland Roads intersect here, and the Stillman Yellow Trail goes through the intersection. You want to turn left on the latter, but to do it, you make a left turn on the road across a bridge for 150 feet to a right fork. The spot is confusing! Immediately on leaving the road at this right fork, the yellow trail makes a sharp left turn through a tall stand of lau-

rel. A gentle climb continues on the right side of high ground, contouring the hill until you see a little rocky knob ahead through the trees. That is the summit of Black Rock at 1,402 feet and two miles from the start, where you will want to pause to enjoy the vista upriver. Yellow-painted footprints on the rock lead you to an opening in which Storm King is framed by Taurus and Beacon.

The continuing yellow route from the summit is most eroded, attesting to the popularity of this section, in contrast to the faint trails you walk in the rest of the forest. You descend to White Oak Road in ten minutes, and turn right on it as it follows the outlet of Arthurs Pond. A lovely swampy vista greets you as you cross a bridge, then head into a plantation of pine. A giant white oak marks the triangle intersection, where you turn left, then in a hundred feet right onto a white-marked trail into a spruce plantation.

A left fork, just after you enter the plantation, would take you to the fire tower summit, but stay on the white trail to pursue a varied nature exploration. This route leads you through a wet sphagnum area with typical bog plants. A large grassy field off to your right is full of frog and bird sounds. The white trail leads you to and along a small dam beside the very pretty impoundment of the Cornwall water system, called Sphagnum Pond. Beyond the pond, the trail crosses Sutherland Road, and here you will turn left on the road toward Sutherland Pond. Go straight ahead on Sutherland Road when Continental Road forks left. Your route will be close to Sutherland Pond for a time with views ahead to rock ledges that dip invitingly to the water. As the

road pulls away from the pond, notice a small path that heads for the shore. It will lead you to one of the rock ledges and a lovely picnic spot, with bird song accompaniment from the marsh at the southern end. By the route outlined, this spot is 1.8 miles from the summit of Black Rock Mountain.

If you look up to your left you will see ledges on the hill above the pond. They are your next destination. To reach them, return to the roadway and continue southwest for 0.2 mile walk to the intersection of Hall Road. Turn right on it at the gate, and in seventy-five feet fork right again onto a blue-marked trail. This leads up a series of ledges to an intersection, where the blue trail turns right and a white trail leads, in just a few hundred feet, to Split Rock with its lovely views of the pond. The white trail continues by turning away from the summit and intersecting the yellow Stillman Trail, which is a right fork; the left fork is the blue trail you just left, and straight ahead is the blue-and-yellow marked route you want. It leads you downhill until the trail splits. The blue would give you a more circuitous return route, but take the yellow which is just as interesting. It shortly intersects a roadway, turning right along it to an intersection with another segment of the Stillman Trail. In less than five minutes, double markers alert you to a left turn that takes you into a lovely laurel stand and across a ridge to yet another intersection. You are back on the Sackett Trail, where yellow circles direct you to the right. Note that yellow squares mark the left fork.

This ridge route leads you to an outcrop with a view before bringing you back to the yellow triangle trail, ten minutes from your car.

11

Schunemunk

Distance: 7 miles
Time: 5 hours
Vertical rise: 1,360 feet
Map: USGS 7½' Cornwall

Schunemunk sits in solitary splendor, its long, gently rounded form isolated from the Hudson Highlands and the Shawangunks as completely as its rocks are separated by ages from their surroundings. Its complexly deformed sedimentary rocks date from the Silurian and Devonian periods, while all around are pre-Silurian formations. The light grayish and pinkish sandstones, shales, and conglomerates that crown its summit were slowly deposited from a landmass to the east. The polished quartz pebbles embedded in the pink and lavender sands could only have been formed by water washing them from the heights of a mountain range. These deposits, the Schunemunk conglomerates, accumulated in a shallow sea. The uplift of the Acadian Orogeny warped and raised this new landmass, so today the conglomerates sit like colored icing on the sandwich of deposits beneath. In addition, the uplift pressed against the long sides of the formation, pushing them up and leaving a deep cleft valley between.

A loop walk from the north will highlight the deep cleft that creases the mountain as well as take you to vantages on both the long eastern and western faces.

To reach the trailhead, drive north on NY 32 from Central Valley to Mountainville and a sign that reads Black Rock Game Club. Here, turn immediately left on Taylor Road, which crosses over the Thruway. On the far side of the crossing, park at a small turnout on the north side of the road. Here a sign notes the easement given by Star Manufacturing Company for hikers to park and walk across the private lands at the foot of the mountain to gain access to its public heights. Hikers are warned that they enter these lands at their own risk and they are cautioned that any use other than hiking is a trespass. Following the example of my companion on this walk, who said that every time he climbed Schunemunk he offered a silent thanks to the owners who have made this access possible, you can show your appreciation by your respect for this property, by observing the regulations that prohibit camping, fires, destruction of flora, and littering.

To make a counterclockwise loop, walk north along the road, noting the yellow blazes on the telephone poles that denote the Jessup Trail. In just short of a mile, past the Taylor home, turn left into the field at the gated entrance. Note that there is no parking here. You walk through the field toward the north end of Schunemunk and at the edge of the woods turn right on a road that leads between posted lands. The yellow blazes, posted signs, and thick poison ivy will keep you from trespassing.

After half a mile, the roadway briefly follows Baby Brook, and about a hundred yards beyond a small waterfall the yellow trail forks right away from the road and up to a railroad track, across those tracks, and into the woods again. The trail continues to climb beside an old stone wall through mountain laurel. If your walk is a spring one, wild oat, spring beauties, and trailing arbutus line the way. Farther along you rejoin the brook where quartz crystals and conglomerates of rounded purple and green rocks brighten the streambed.

You climb about 700 feet in just over a mile to arrive at an intersection. Here, about an hour into the trip, the Western Ridge Trail, marked with blue dots on a white rectangle, forks right across Baby Brook to begin the climb of the western ridge. This scramble, over pinkish conglomerates, zigzags quickly up so that within a few minutes you can enjoy views back over Storm King and Black Rock Forest. As you climb higher, the panorama of Beacon and Newburgh Bay on the Hudson emerges. Near the top of the knifelike edge of the western ridge, views northwest to the Gunks and Catskills begin, and you have your first glimpse of the eastern ridge.

You pass a trail intersection, but many

markings do not quite conform to previous guides. However, it is easy to follow the route along the ridge. There seems to be an intermix of the turquoise-blue of the Long Path and the white-with-red that should only denote the Barton Swamp Trail, which breaks off just after the intersection near Baby Brook to wind through the cleft. Stay on the ridge, in any case, and for about forty-five minutes you can enjoy the openness of the walk, the views of the eastern ridge, and occasional openings to the west. After nearly two miles along the ridge, blue markers as well as the white-with-red direct you left for a brief descent into the moist realm of the cleft, which you follow south briefly. The red trail continues south, but you want a blue-marked left fork, which shortly begins to climb the eastern ridge. This scramble will take you in twenty minute to intersect again the Jessup Trail with its yellow markers. Here you turn north, left, to complete the loop. This ridge is broader, more heavily wooded, with fewer views, although from the peak at 1,664 feet you can see the northern end of Harriman Park.

Just beyond the peak, yellow arrows on the rock slabs point you west to the megaliths, columns of pink and white conglomerate split off from the ridge. Besides the beauty of the spot, your three hours' walk to this point makes it a good lunch spot.

A fifteen-minute walk north along the trail brings you to the spot where the Dark Hollow Restored Trail forks right, white-with-black marks. You can take it down if you choose, for it intersects the way to be described near the base of the mountain. In fact, you may wish to return to walk this alternate trail, as well as others along Schunemunk's crest. For now, continue on the yellow trail along the ridgetop with its pink and purple conglomerate slabs, a color fantasy of gray-green lichens on mauve. The gleaming white quartz pebbles shine like precious stones.

You will also find two places with views in this just-over-a-mile-long portion of trail, which you can cover in less than half an hour. The next intersection brings you to a right fork onto the white-marked Sweet Clover Trail. Here a sign designates the distance south along the Jessup, but no mention of the nearly 2.5 miles along which you will follow this trail to your car.

The forty-minute descent is punctuated by tantalizing sounds of rushing water from the hemlock-concealed stream in Dark Hollow, but there are no views into it. The trail emerges beside the railroad tracks, fifty yards north of the cairn that marks the end of the Dark Hollow Trail. Go straight across the tracks and intersect a dirt road, back on private land. The road leads you along the western edge of a field, then across it and beside a farm to emerge on Taylor Road opposite your car.

East of the
Hudson

Ruins of a stone church on Dennytown Road

Fahnestock State Park

Distance: 7.5 miles
Time: 4½ hours
Vertical rise: Less than 500 feet
Map: USGS 7½' Oscawana Lake; NY–NJTC East Hudson
   Trails, #15

Fahnestock State Park, astride the Taconic Parkway in Putnam County, has several lovely lakes, a huge swimming pool, and picnic and boating facilities. It also has many miles of trails that will take you far from the crowds that regularly enjoy the park. Perhaps the best introduction to Fahnestock's quieter areas is a figure-eight walk that loops around its southern hills and ridges. The park, begun with the gift in 1929 of Dr. Alfred Fahnestock in memory of his father, Dr. Clarence Fahnestock, and added to in the 1960s, now totals 6,200 acres.

West of the Taconic Parkway on NY 301 is one of the park's prettier lakes, Canopus. There are two parking areas near it, and opposite the western one, on the south side of the road, you will see an old roadway. Walk along it, and you will easily pick up the blue trail markers that quickly lead you south into a deep forest of tremendously tall hemlock. The trail begins by following an old roadway, with tailings of an abandoned mine on your right. The mines in this area, especially Sunk Mine, which you will walk near shortly, provided ore to the West Point Foundry at Cold Spring. This ore, with ore from the Greenwood Mines, was turned into the Parrot guns of the Union

Army artillery. The bed of the railroad built in 1862 to carry ore from the mines makes the handsome route you will follow at the end of this walk.

All the land about you was purchased by Adolphe Philipse in 1691 and established as the Philipse Grant six years later by King William III. The vast and rugged wilderness surrounding the interior range of hills could not be farmed and never had many settlers. Only the eight-mile-long vein of iron ore that follows the ridgeline of the hills south managed to attract settlers and then not until after 1800. Even the early miners regarded these dark woods as foreboding; actually, because they have not been logged for many years, the woods probably look now very much as they did then.

The first mine you pass, identifiable only by its tailings pit, belonged to Richard Hopper who opened it in 1820. It remained a small operation until the Civil War when Philipse heirs sold the mineral rights to Paul S. Forbes, the builder of the railway. The mining survived until the panic of 1873, and the surrounding land was obtained by Dr. Clarence Fahnestock in 1915 after a series of intervening land sales.

Beyond the tailings, you will see a lovely marsh with lots of birds. In less than half a mile you reach the first fork; the roadway continues straight, you turn right past fields of hay-scented fern and down to a charming little brook. Again, tall hemlocks cool the small ravine. Here, the trail crosses the brook and arcs back north along the stream almost to a meadow before it turns left, uphill. A zig-zag in the trail brings you to a ridge in the impressive forest, certainly one of the more handsome second-growth forests in southern New York.

It will have taken no more than thirty-five minutes to walk the mile-plus distance to the intersection with the white-marked Appalachian Trail. Cross it and continue on the blue trail, watching for Hidden Lake on your right. You may want to wander off the trail to examine this manmade pond, filled with stumps. With its dam breached, it has a wierd, desolate appearance. At the south end of the lake, you will find a road that detours to the dam.

You continue on a ridge, and barely sense marshy Sunk Mine Pond, again on your right. Thirty minutes from the AT crossing, you cross the outlet of this second pond. Here the trail may confuse you, for it forks right to rejoin the road-way, while other hikers have beaten a path straight ahead toward a marshy area. The road, which you will follow atop a causeway, reaches the outlet dam, from which you have your first good view of the pond.

Time has altered the features of the mines and ponds, but a nineteenth century observer once wrote about a spot not far from here that was the destination of an 1887 picnic. The trip to Pine Swamp was described by E. M. Hopkins, one of the picnickers who spent a summer afternoon exploring the Sunk Mine, an enormous cleft "gently filled with green slimey looking water." All the ac-cessible ore had been removed, and "one end of the cleft terminates at the surface of the sloap; for the other a lateral drift, whose mouth is partly con-cealed by water extends into the moun-tains . . . None now living can remember when it was in operation." Two picnickers entered the mine guided by dry birch bark torches. Inside they discovered the canoe of one Levi Marshall, deceased, who had claimed once to have found a silver mine. Thinking they had discovered Marshall's lost silver mine, they walked deeper and deeper into the mine, until they found a pile of silver objects, teapots, plates, and other objects. Lead-ing up from the cache was a ladder that led the picnickers into Marshall's cabin. The residents at the time were charged with burglary, putting an end to the rumors that silver could be mined with the iron in these hills.

After crossing the outlet of Sunk Mine Pond on a bridge below the spillway, you climb to Sunk Mine Road, marked also with white blazes. Walk right 200 yards along the roadway until you see the double blue makers of your trail. Here a left turn onto the blue trail takes you uphill to a ridge, then along the rock outcrops atop the ridge. The final outcrop with a through-the-trees view is a good spot for lunch after a two-hour walk.

The trail follows a narrow trench down-hill to another marsh. Triple blazes direct you to turn right and walk along its west-ern side. Gorgeous maples shade the head of the marsh. Here, the trail enters the woods again, crosses a stream on a small bridge and emerges in a field be-side the ruins of a stone church. The trail now follows Dennytown Road south for 0.4 mile before it enters the woods again. Watch for the white AT markers here, and also watch where you walk because of the dense thickets of poison ivy. You make a left turn, then quickly a second acute-angled left turn onto the trail, which

heads down through a locust grove and into the woods along the stone walls of an abandoned settlement whose first residents were the Dennys, miners of the southern portion of the vein.

After crossing the outlet of Beaver Pond which you glimpse through the trees, you will wind up and down ridges for about a mile until the trail meets and follows an abandoned roadway steeply down into a hemlock gorge. Here, after 1.5 miles on the AT, you cross the road again and head past stone foundations toward the outlet of Sunk Mine Lake. You may want to pause and enjoy the waterfall in this small gem of a gorge, which you reach after a slow hour's walk from the lunch stop. In this area, you will several times cross a red-marked horse trail.

Next you climb to a blueberry knob with no real views and head again down into a hemlock ravine. Beyond lie apple trees and the small grassy meadows of an abandoned home site. The trail continues briefly beside a stream, then heads up a ridge to cross the blue trail, 1.2 miles north of Sunk Mine Road.

About a quarter-mile beyond, the trail joins the bed of a narrow gauge railway. Admire the wonderful rockwork that carried the rails around a semicircular causeway at the head of a ravine. All too quickly the trail emerges on the roadway a hundred yards west of the place you began.

Pawling Nature Reserve

Distance: 7.2 miles
Time: 4 hours
Vertical rise: 700 feet
Maps: USGS 7½′ Pawling, NY–CT; USGS 7½′ Dover Plains,
  NY–CT

The Appalachian Trail traverses Hammersly Ridge through the thousand-acre Pawling Nature Reserve. Combining it with a walk on Quaker Road and some of the Reserve's other trails makes not only a fair hike, but also gives a delightful chance to observe a variety of flora from a deep hemlock gorge to wet meadows and swamps.

Two trailheads for the reserve are on Quaker Lake Road, north of Quaker Lake. To reach them, turn east off NY 22 north of Pawling at Hurd Corners, and continue on County Route 68 for 1.5 miles to Baker Corner, where you turn left on Quaker Lake Road. A figure-eight walk through the Reserve can be started at the southern parking lot, 1.3 miles north on Quaker Lake Road, just beyond the private lands of Quaker Lake.

A yellow-marked trail from this lot immediately enters the gorge with its charming waterfall and lush ferns. The trail continues briefly beside the stream and crosses it (on a challenging log) before mounting the rocky slopes of the ridge. In a half mile, the trail swings north along the ridge, then intersects the white-marked Appalachian Trail at an acute angle. Your continuing route north has both yellow and white markers. Pinkster flowers, a variety of ferns, and marsh plants fill the wet areas along the ridgetop, areas that were cleared and farmed sometime before the Revolutionary War. In 0.3 mile a red trail forks right, but you should continue on the yellow and white trail for twenty minutes more, about 0.9 mile, along the ridgeline.

Where the white AT goes straight ahead, you take the yellow trail for 0.3 mile down the eastern slope of the ridge. The trail crosses the outlet of Quaker Lake where it turns right to emerge at the northern parking area. Here turn right again to follow Quaker Lake Road south through the valley for just under a mile. Almost within sight of a house with a pond, two red blazes alert you to turn right again, and cross the stream on a small footbridge. Beyond it you will scramble up the junglelike growth of the hillside to reach the ridge again, then follow the red trail as it angles left to intersect the white and yellow trail. This red segment is one mile long.

Turn left on the 0.3 mile yellow-and-white segment, which you walk this time in a southerly direction. At the intersection with the AT, turn right onto it to climb a short ridge. Near the top of the ridge, watch closely, for the trail makes a

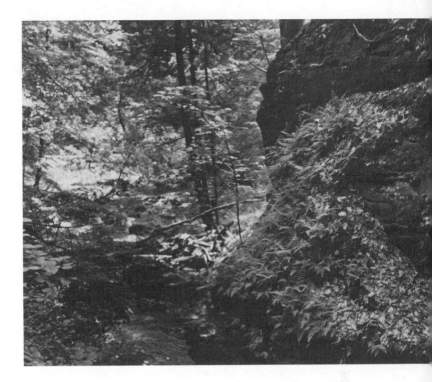

Fern glen in Pawling Nature Reserve

sharp left turn. Others obviously have missed this turn before you, for there is a well-worn path into an upland swamp, in spite of the Nature Conservancy's warning to stay on the trail and avoid trampling the fragile wet meadow areas. The route continues through a handsome open forest along the ridge, gradually descending into a spruce plantation and emerging on Quaker Lake Road. This 1.9 mile walk beyond the red trail takes about forty-five minutes. Here you turn left, north, and you can walk back to your car in twenty minutes easily.

14

Mills–Norrie State Parks

Distance: 5 miles
Time: 3 hours
Vertical rise: Minimal
Maps: Available from Taconic State Park Region Headquarters, Mills–Norrie State Parks, Staatsburg; USGS 7½' Hyde Park

The east shore of the Hudson River between New York and Albany was settled by holders of large patents and purchases. Portions of a few of these magnificent holdings survive as modern parks. In the mid-Hudson Valley, the most beautiful of these parks are the great homes and estates, built in the nineteenth century. Some, like the Vanderbilt Mansion and the Mills Estate, were the homes of industrial and financial leaders of the time. Clermont, the home of many generation of Livingstons, a family including notable statesmen, dates to the eighteenth century. Frederic Edwin Church, the Hudson River School painter, designed the grounds of his Persian-influenced castle, Olana, to frame the vistas of the distant Catskills.

Each of these parks has walks laid out by the original owners. Most are short and through manicured grounds. The walks along the Hudson at the Mills–Norrie State Parks are special: they are longer, offering a half day of outdoor activity, and a portion are directly along the river, for the railroad, which closely follows the eastern shore through most of the valley, lies inland here.

The Mills estate was built by a great-great-granddaughter of Robert R. Livingston, Ruth Livingston Mills, and her husband, Ogden Mills, a wealthy financier. The Greek revival mansion, which was designed by the firm of McKim, Mead and White, was completed in 1896. The Louis XV and Louis XVI rooms were richly furnished with art from Europe, ancient Greece, and the Orient.

The estate's formal sweep of lawn and its treecovered roadway offer a charming beginning to the trails that lead south to the adjacent Margaret Lewis Norrie State Park. To reach the Mills estate, turn onto Old Post Road, which loops west from NY 9 around the village of Staatsburg. You will want to stop at the park offices in the mansion and get a map, although the ski-touring map available there does not show the shore-hugging route that is the centerpiece of this walk. You can follow its red, blue and green trails on your own.

Walk west from the estate on the blue trail, following the roadway toward the waterfront boathouse, enjoying views of the Catskills on the way. The boathouse, architecturally interesting in itself, is a barrel-vaulted stone structure. The roadway curves around the cove beyond; watch for the white-marked trail that forks right to hug the shoreline. Along it, hem-

Hudson River

ULSTER CO
DUTCHESS CO

ave
pint

P
Mills Mansion

CONRAIL

RO

50

Golf Course

94

Barn

MILLS

STATE

Staatsburg
(BM 30)

MEMORIAL

PARK

Main hiking route
(including ski trails)
Other ski trails

95

Rus

Vira

OLD POST

RD

Picnic
Area

RIVER

84

BM
31

Union
Sch

Old Post Road

50

Indian

NY Route 9

45

Conrail Right-of-Way

62

Norrie Heights

N

Tower

NORRIE STATE PARK

1

50

100

Cat

Lights

BM
22

0   0.5   1.0 mile

200

43

Norrie
Point

Norrie Point Environmental Museum

locks shade the small shale cliffs bordering the river with its shingle beach. The
narrow trail follows the top of moss-
covered ledges, while you have lovely
views of water and gnarled cedars. Only
an occasional old stone wall will make
you believe this land has ever been dis-
turbed by man.

A forty-minute walk brings you to a picnic area, (which also can be reached by
a roadway from Norrie Park). The white-
marked route continues on the far (south)
side of the parking area, but farther inland, leading through a camping area to
a roadway. Follow that roadway out until
it intersects another park road, not far
from the railroad. South on the park
road, in about an hour's total walk, you
reach the Dutchess Community College
Environmental Museum, open Saturdays
from 11 to 5 and Sundays from 1 to 5.
You may want to see its exhibits of the
plants and animals of this portion of the
Hudson shoreline.

As you return north along the road,
watch for an underpass below the railroad. Opposite it, a red post along the
road alerts you to an abandoned roadway that serves as one of the park's unmarked trails. Follow this to the left, as it
curves back and then almost disappears
on the summit of a small hill with a stone
water tower. There are a multitude of
such walkways in the park, some of
which shortly will be marked as nature
trails.

Following this one, you intersect one of
the park roads (blue) that has been
marked as a ski-touring route. Your route
back north to the Mills estate can take
any one of the intersecting segments of
the ski trails, most of which follow abandoned roadways, but for now follow the
blue trail to a T intersection, where you
turn left on the red trail.

Your detour through the woods takes
you past a marsh, through beautiful
forests, and to a memorial pylon noting
that this land was given to the people of
Staatsburg in memory of Lewis Gordon
Norrie, 1901–1923. Just beyond the
pylon, turn left, following the ski-touring
signs. As the park map indicates, these
trails all lead back to the large barn near
the point where the white trail headed
along the shore. To extend your walk,
you may wish to choose different segments of the loop; they are clearly
marked and easy to follow. A most
delightful way to end the day is with a
picnic on the lawn in front of the
mansion.

Stissing Mountain and Thompson Pond

Distance: 4 miles
Time: 4 hours
Vertical rise: 950 feet
Map: USGS 7½′ Pine Plains

Stissing Mountain's long profile so dominates the surrounding flattened fields that it appears taller than its 1,403-foot height would indicate. The fields, remnants of a glacial lake, encircle this dome of Precambrian gneiss, enhancing the mountain's scale. A pair of trails leads to the abandoned fire tower summit, making a loop walk possible, although views are limited to openings in the forest cover. A companion walk around Thompson Pond on the west below the mountain makes this a lovely short day's excursion. The pond is part of a kettle lake, formed with Stissing and Mud Ponds to the north by the melting of glacial blocks. Now the resulting bogpond, filling with grasses and cattails, is home to many birds. From the path that winds along its shores, you can not only watch those birds, but you also will be treated to views of Stissing across the marshes, as the mountain rises steeply from the level of the lake bed.

The mountain is unusual in that its Precambrian mass was thrust on much younger sandstones and shales that form the surrounding valley, completely isolating it from similar landforms that make up the Ramapos and the Hudson Highlands. Its strong profile that dominates the coun-

tryside is due to resistance of the Precambrian rocks to erosion.

The pond and 300 acres are managed as a preserve by the Nature Conservancy. It is home to many mammals, migrating warblers and marsh birds, and a rich variety of plants that find their niche in areas as varied as the pond and the adjacent wooded slopes of Stissing Mountain.

To reach the trailhead, start at the intersection of NY 82 and 199 in Pine Plains, and drive south for 0.4 mile on NY 82. A right turn on Lake Road takes you out of the village, along a lovely stretch of maple-lined road and across a causeway, 1.6 miles to the Thompson Pond Sanctuary entrance on the left. The trailhead for Stissing Mountain is unmarked and 0.2 mile farther, near a bend in the road where the shoulder is wide enough for parking.

There is little or no marking on the trail, but it is easy to follow. The 950-foot climb should take you less than forty minutes. It begins steeply up a narrow path that intersects an abandoned roadway, which you will meet after a five-minute climb. Turn left, for the way right leads to private lands, and continue uphill. Another five-minute walk brings you

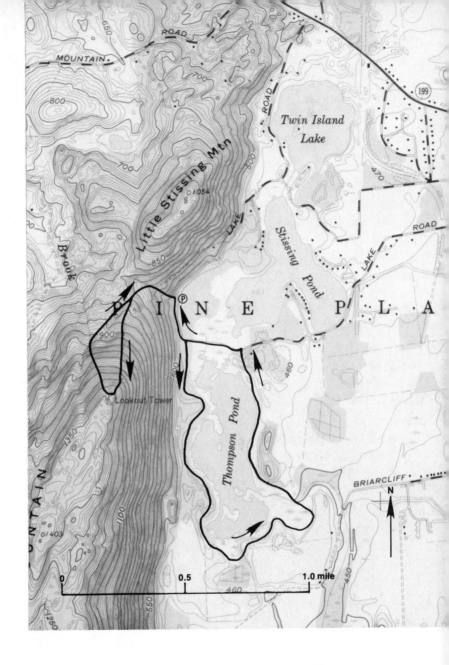

to a fork. The way right, marked with a red arrow as the trail, follows the old roadway and is the much more obvious choice. You will return that way.

Take the left turn to a faint and fairly steep path. Stones heaped beside the trail indicate this too was once a cleared way, but it is now rubble-filled and eroded. You can see Stissing Pond occasionally through the scrub oaks and birches, tantalizing glimpses that finally open up, after a thirty-minute walk, to re-

veal the northern hills. These are the best views the mountain offers. The summit is overgrown, and the fire tower stairs have been removed. The foundations of a cabin lie below the tower on the narrow summit ridge.

Walk beside the tower, heading south on a faint path. The descent is simple if you keep bearing right; left always leads to private lands. The first choice is within a hundred yards of the tower, and the way right is steeply down to intersect an abandoned roadway in another hundred yards. Here a right continues downhill following the roadway past handsome rock ledges. Below the ledges and another right fork, you can see Little Stissing Mountain through the trees. A thirty-five-minute walk brings you back to the fork you passed on the ascent. Retrace your steps for the ten-minute walk to your car, completing the 1.5-mile circuit.

To add to the excursion, walk along the road to the Thompson Pond Sanctuary entrance. An old road leads you south into the sanctuary, and 200 yards from the road is a registration booth and a map of the sanctuary. You scarcely need a map for the counterclockwise walk around Thompson Pond. There is a short loop to the pond from the registration booth marked with blue arrows. The main trail around the pond, marked with yellow, continues on the abandoned roadway. The only time you might have trouble is at the far southern end where the trail leads briefly to a weed-filled field. Head left along the fence, and the way will soon become obvious again. The trail continues near the sanctuary border, heading down into a swamp toward a decrepit boardwalk. The swamp, outlet of Thompson Pond, marks the headwaters of Wappingers Creek. Lovely views of Stissing follow, then the trail cuts again to the border fence circling around another swampy area, taking you briefly to the edge of a barnyard. The trail then heads back closer to the pond for the rest of the return to Lake Road. An hour or so will take you around the 2.5-mile circuit. With binoculars you will surely want to take longer. There is also a rich variety of ground cover to examine and a series of framed views of marsh and mountain to enjoy.

South Taconic Trail

Distance: 9 miles
Time: 7 hours
Vertical rise: More than 2,000 feet
Maps: NYSDT Copake; USGS 7½′ Copake, NY–MA; USGS
 7½′ Bashbish Falls, MA–CT–NY

A sentinel line of hills forms the border between New York State and Massachusetts and Connecticut. A fifteen-mile range trail follows the crest, paralleling the border, much of the time in New York State. This most eastern of New York's great trails is a relative newcomer, built between 1972 and 1976 by Bob Redington and Frank Cary, both residents of Connecticut. This hike takes you on a portion of that trail system, from Whitehouse Road in the south to the magnificent Bashbish Falls in the north. The route encompasses a chain of vantages that will inspire any hiker and make light the rigors of the long walk with its many climbs.

The Taconics are remnants of a thrust mass of mostly unmetamorphosed shales ranging from Cambrian to Middle Ordovician in age. The ancestral Taconics, products of violent upheavals known as the Taconic Orogeny, became eroded away; sands and gravels from the mountains were washed west into a sea whose waves deposited a thick layer of the quartz-pebble conglomerate whose later upthrust became the Shawangunks. By Late Silurian times only the eroded vestiges of the original Taconic Mountains remained. And fine muds and limestones

again accumulated in a shallow sea, forming the bed of Upper Silurian limestone near Pine Plains and beneath Stissing Mountain. From overlooks on the Taconic Ridge, this quiet plain contrasts vividly with the forces that created the mountains on which you will walk.

Because of the length of the walk and the advantages of staying on the ridge, a two-car trip is best. To leave one car at the north, turn east from NY 22 at Copake Falls onto NY 344, and drive through Bashbish Park to a parking area on the south side of the road 1.4 miles from NY 22.

In the south, take Whitehouse Road, an east turn from NY 22, 5.5 miles north of the traffic light in Millerton, and turn left again in 0.7 mile. A right turn in 0.3 mile leads in 0.9 mile to a small parking turnout. White square marks denote the trail, which begins across the edge of the field. The gentle uphill toward the looming mountain quickly ends in 0.4 mile in a scramble beside a small stream. In half a mile the trail reaches a tall but scanty waterfall. Then, the trail turns and zigzags up the steep face, yielding views along the northern escarpment of the Taconics and south to Stissing Mountain, with the Gunks and Beacon beyond.

Bash Bish Falls

Within thirty minutes the scrambling ends, and you reach a sign pointing 0.7 mile back the way you just climbed, 0.18 mile to the right to New Point to a lookout, a detour from the projected route, and 1.24 miles ahead to Brace Mountain. Continue on to Brace, past a couple of nice openings with pretty views, then as the trail turns again to the mountain, you climb a pair of ledges to reach South Brace and a vantage with views south over New Point and Riga Lake and South Pond beyond. Here, at 1.4 miles, a turquoise trail forks back to Riga, a possible loop route for another day.

About an hour and a quarter from the start, you reach the summit of South Brace, 2,304 feet, with its superb views. Beyond, the summit continues open with small birches and oaks. You drop into a saddle, then climb to a huge cairn monument on the summit of Brace, 2,311 feet, from which there is a 360-degree view. From this point, nearly two miles from the

start, you see Bear Mountain, the highest point in Connecticut, to the east and Mount Frissell in Massachusetts to the northeast. The split summit of Mount Adams is on the horizon ahead.

Continuing north, the trail descends about 350 yards to intersect a woods road. The way right leads into Connecticut; your trail continues north, joining the old, shingle-filled road, which follows along the narrow ridge to a signpost pointing to Mount Frissell and the tri-state marker. From here it is 3.71 miles to Alander Mountain. Just beyond this spot you pass a lovely upland pond and continue down, then up to another knob.

Beyond, the trail descends, fairly steeply, crossing into Massachusetts. A side trail left heads toward Boston Corner and another beyond heads right to Ashley Mountain. Your route north continues on the old roadway, bordered with stone walls.

After you pass a gorge with a small stream on your left and enter a park-like area of tall trees, you will see a red marker denoting a trail joining from Robert Brook and Boston Corner to the west. This intersection is two miles from the summit of Brace. The trail continues with red markers for about a ten-minute, half-mile walk to a fork where a blue trail turns right toward the summit of Alander Mountain, which you can gain by either this blue route or a continuation of the trail you have been following. On the blue trail it takes about twenty minutes to pass through scrubby forests to open ledges. There are lovely green fields of the Harlem Valley beneath and views back to the cairn on Brace. You circle west to the summit, past a series of strange convoluted ledges and a cleft with a cabin from the days when the fire tower on Alander was manned. It is a fairly leisurely four-hour walk for the six miles to Alander.

From the summit itself, 2,240 feet, you view the hemlock-rimmed valley of Alander Brook. West of the summit there is a point from which the capitol in Albany appears against the skyline. To the east of the tower there is a fork in the trail, with marks painted on a rock. Take the blue trail, which leads quickly to the white trail north along the very precipitous northeast ridge of Alander. The descent is fairly steep as it follows the narrow ridge, crossing to the west to overlook a bucolic scene of farm fields and little ponds.

The trail continues high on the ridge-line, descending slightly, occasionally climbing little knobs, punctuated with many lovely view spots. The high point of Bashbish Mountain at 1,980 feet is just under two miles from Alander. Just beyond, after fifty minutes of winding across the ridge, you reach an intersection.

Choose carefully here. The way left avoids fording the brook, but does not take you past Bashbish Falls. Instead it leads you to a bridge over the brook, and you would have to backtrack through the park to see this choicest part of the trip. If the water is not too high and cold, and probably that would be only in early spring, you can turn right for a wild descent through the hemlock-covered slopes at what seems to be a 70-degree angle. In less than half a mile, the trail takes you down to the railing that keeps you from falling into the gorge. It is a rough descent, but the views of the falls from this side are worth the trip. You continue descending past several tiers of falls that break through the ravine as the brook ends its plunge down 700 feet of this cleft in the Taconic ridge. The falls lie just over the New York border in Massachusetts. Fording the stream just below the falls will lead you up to the stairs constructed on the north side for more sedate viewing of this cataract. The park road leads you along the rim of the gorge and in fifteen minutes to your car.

17

Olana

Distance: 7 miles
Time: 3 hours
Vertical rise: 300 feet
Maps: Available from the ticket office at Olana

As the romanticism of nineteenth-century Hudson River School painting is exemplified in the works of Frederic Edwin Church (1826–1900), the belief that nature could be manipulated to express that romanticism is summarized in Church's home, Olana. The Olana State Historic Site near Hudson preserves the grounds Church designed and the castle he built that surveys the Catskills and a bend in the Hudson River. Now, a century later, a walk through the grounds and a tour of the castle summarize those romantic notions of nature as eloquently as any river site or any painting.

Olana is on NY 9G, just south of the entrance to the Rip Van Winkle Bridge between Hudson and Catskill. The park grounds are open from dawn to dusk throughout the year. Tours of the castle are offered Wednesday through Sunday from noon to four o'clock from Memorial Day through the last Sunday in October. There is a nominal fee of $.50 for the tour.

Frederic Edwin Church studied with Thomas Cole and painted Hudson River and Catskill scenes throughout his career. For two decades, he traveled throughout the west, to Newfoundland, and to South America. In 1867 he and his wife visited Greece, Italy, and Syria. was the architectural styles of the latter country that inspired the pink stone castle that his wife named Olana, a Latin interpretation of a Syrian word meaning "our place on high."

Olana sits on a narrow ridge 500 feet above the Hudson, a site that inspired Church to write, "about one hour this side of Albany is the center of the world—I own it." The magnificent trees that now edge the sweeping lawn have grown to full maturity, as have the oaks and maples that shade the carriage roads making up the park's trails. From the castle, the view southwest encompasses the northern escarpment of the Catskills, the bend in the Hudson, and a lake Church had constructed as a necessary artistic counterpoint to complete the dramatic view. The castle's windows were designed to frame portions of that view, enabling its owners to command in nature a view as awe-inspiring as Church's painted scenes.

A walk on portions of the 7.5 miles of trails and carriage roads is more of an elegant stroll than a hike, but you can extend it through two lovely loops. A trail enters the woods just below and east of the road to the visitors' parking area. A left fork near the beginning takes you onto Ridge Road, which winds to the north and then below the castle with one vista of the river and the Rip Van Winkle

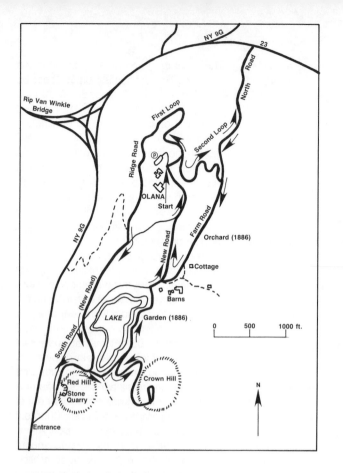

Bridge. Follow Ridge Road, marked with yellow disks, as it circles to the park entrance road (South Road), which you follow downhill (south) toward the lake. Turn left from South Road along the lake. The first right from this trail leads to the southern park boundary. This route continues on private lands along a very narrow ridge that affords glimpses of the Hudson.

Returning to the lake trail, continue north along the lake, enjoying occasional glimpses of the hilltop castle. The next right turn, red-marked, leads to a circle on the summit of Crown Hill, where a cut in the forest reveals the castle again. The entire park is full of such surprising, yet planned, vistas. The lake trail ends at a roadway (marked New Road on map) along which you can make your way

north to the castle.

A second loop also begins near the parking area, but goes to the right (south) down through a deep ravine of stately trees to the North Road. Follow this north to the park boundary and back to enjoy more of the noble forest. Retracing the route south to continue on Farm Road, you remain on the ridge overlooking the old orchards. You may wish to turn west from the roads and wind generally west and uphill through the fields toward the castle. If you do, be wary of the poison ivy patches. Near the intersection of the two paved park roads, a pathway circles below the castle and leads gently up to it via a small but charming Victorian garden that is tucked just below the castle garden wall.

The Shawangunks

The Trapps to Gertrude's Nose

Distance: 8.5 miles
Time: 6 hours
Vertical rise: 800 feet
Maps: USGS 7½' Gardiner; USGS 7½' Napanoch; NY–NJTC
   Shawangunk Trails, #9

The long ridge edged with sparkling white cliffs visible to the west of the New York State Thruway in the vicinity of New Paltz is Shawangunks, pronounced Shongum. For a first look at this geologically intriguing spot, try the hike along the Trapps, a portion of those cliffs, to Gertrude's Nose. Drive west of New Paltz on NY 299 to NY 44 and 55, and continue west to park along the shoulder of the road near the cliffs, which usually are full of rock climbers. Your route will take you southwest along the cliff tops on a trip that for a nonrock climber is as much of a thrill as the climbers get from those famous cliffs, know worldwide as the "Gunks."

Because your route starts on lands belonging to the Mohonk Preserve, there is a fee, $2.00 per person as of this writing, usually collected by a ranger who patrols the road. The crowds whose vehicles line the road are climbers; you will meet very few hikers on your walk. The Mohonk Preserve office is located on Mountain Rest Road near New Paltz, and there you will find much information on the natural history of the area, a part of which is described in a wonderful little booklet

On the trail to Gertrude's Nose, view southwest

that you may wish to purchase.

Walk just south of Trapps Bridge, over which the carriage road from Minnewaska to Mohonk passes, and follow that road northwest for about a hundred feet. Here a well-marked blue trail starts steeply up the rock slabs to the Millbrook Ridge Trail.

The beauty of the Shawangunks lies in the way the views continuously unfold, enlivening every few feet of each walk. Still, a sparkling day in early spring or late fall with the leaves off and not too much wind is the best for this hike. You will be walking along a knife edge, sometimes so narrow you feel a good gust could give you flight, like the birds you will see soaring close by.

You are immediately aware of the cleft in the Shawangunk ridge—you will walk the eastern ridge until it meets the western one near Minnewaska, a resort whose lands once encompassed most of the central Shawangunks. As you climb you see the cliffs and tower of Mohonk, a hotel whose grounds, together with the Mohonk Preserve lands, make up the northern Shawangunks. These cliffs and the tower of Sky Top frame the high peaks of the central Catskill range—a view that will return many times during this walk.

It is the rock under your feet and what you know of its history that will most impress you on this walk. The Shawangunks were formed about 450 million years ago, first as sedimentary deposits worn from an even older mountain range. The sediments, the shining white conglomerates you now see, were once deposited along the shores of an inland sea, whose waters tumbled and smoothed the quartz pebbles, which were later imbedded in the gleaming white rocks you will traverse. These sediments were shaped by heat and pressure, faulted and bent, and uplifted about 280 million years ago to form the magnificent cliffs of the Shawangunks' southwestern face, where the horizontal layers of deposits are worn away. The dip to the northwest gives the long slopes you see; these slopes will be even more evident if you take the Ice Caves of the Shawangunks hike. The age of the uplift makes the Shawangunks one of the younger formations in the east.

So, let's begin the walk along the straight, thin ridges of the sloping face of the Shawangunks' geological history. Scrub oak and pitch pine will be your companions, opening up to offer a series of beautiful vistas along the way.

You climb a first rise, the site of the annual hawk watches, then descend into a little draw, climbing again, this time more sharply, to turn left and return to the exposed slopes of the amazingly narrow ridge. The trail is routed along bare rock as much as possible, minimizing erosion of the fragile niches of blueberries and laurels. You zigzag across the ridge to take advantage of the rock walkways and the views, but the lack of evidence of defined foot tread means you need to watch for the trail markers. With your eyes diverted to distant views, it is easy to wander off the trail.

A half-hour walk through a section of taller trees with few views brings you to a deeper valley. As you climb again, you see Millbrook Mountain looming ahead like Gibraltar. About an hour's walk brings you past a big rock slab, cantilevered to create a shelter. Then, passing another protected area of larger hemlock, you scramble left to circle to the edge of the cliffs once more. You look down now on Heddens Lake, whose position will mark your progress through the walk. The view south down the Hudson Highlands reveals Breakneck Ridge and Storm King, while toward the north the Catskills are framed by the cliffs you have just climbed. Observe how the Minnewaska Ridge to the northwest grows closer—when it connects with the Trapp Ridge you are on, their joint thrust forms the prong of Gertrude's Nose, your ultimate destination.

An hour and forty minutes of walking should bring you to the high point of Millbrook Mountain, a wonderfully narrow ridge where the trail emerges several times right at cliff top. The route west continues on a height of land, 1,200 feet above the valley, and twenty minutes later you reach the end of Mohonk property and encounter the loop that marks the end of the Millbrook Mountain carriage road from Minnewaska, about 2.5 miles from the start. For now, take the carriage road. It is easy walking, a bit dull, but the quickest way to make a loop walk around Gertrude's Nose. The carriage roads are the marvel of Mohonk and Minnewaska, miles and miles of graded pathways that today make superb walking. They all are paved with the Martinsburg shale, a 2,000-foot layer of which underlies the Shawangunks. The shale weathers to a dense but surprisingly soft and smooth walking surface. Except on the trails, you will be unaware of the shale, for it is almost everywhere topped with the white icing of the conglomerate.

It takes just over half an hour to cover

N

the mile to an intersection with a red-marked trail that leaves the carriage road on your left. Yellow flags may also alert you to the red trail. Follow it as it descends toward the Palmaghatt Ravine, the deep ravine between you and Castle Point. The ravine was the site of a "salted" gold mine, which deceived several investors nearly a century ago.

For a time, the trail is along the edge of hemlock-covered ledges, sometimes on the white sloping slabs of the cliff tops yielding views ahead to Gertrude's Nose. A twenty-minute walk brings you to an opening under telephone lines and across a little stream.

As you head out to the white slabs you will have to stop and admire some of the glacial erratics that dot the cliff tops. Observe also the deep clefts that fissure the cliffs, created as the soft shale foundations weathered and became displaced. The fifty minutes it may take you to walk the mile from the carriage road to the Nose includes time for you to pause to admire the sculptured rock wonders. Here the evidence of another geological force is clear: the glaciers that once covered the Shawangunks to a depth of four to five thousand feet. As the ice mass moved along the northwestern slopes, the rocks it pushed along scraped the conglomerate, leaving striations, long thin scratch marks that you can see occasion-

ally. The smooth polish of many surfaces is also the work of the glaciers, achieved as the ice mass moved over a layer of mud.

Pause at the promontory of Gertrude's Nose for lunch and views to the east. When you start south along the ridge you will follow some old brown markers and newer red ones. The way is not well-marked as of this writing, mostly because of fire disturbance — a reminder that no fires are permitted in the entire fragile Shawangunk area. Rerouting and remarking is scheduled, so these cautions on trail location may be unnecessary. The way is close enough to the escarpment edge that you will have several good views east and north and even on toward Millbrook Mountain. In little more than half an hour you pass under the power lines, then climb again along ledges amid stunted trees and rocks that form a landscape reminiscent of wind-swept tropical islands. Just over half an hour's walking should bring you out to the carriage road a few minutes from that road's end. The time for this 1.5 mile loop on the Nose may be increased if you have difficulty finding the trail. About an hour and forty minutes should suffice for the return trip to your car, providing you do not stop too long to savor the views.

Minnewaska Scenic Trail

Distance: 11 miles
Time: 7 hours
Vertical Rise: 600 feet, plus scrambles
Maps: USGS 7½′ Gardiner; USGS 7½′ Napanoch; NY–NJTC
  Shawangunk Trails, #9

Minnewaska's Scenic Trail offers a great walk that combines the best of the Minnewaska carriage roads with interconnecting paths that take you on a moderately strenuous but wonderfully varied trip.

Minnewaska State Park is limited to day use only. Its public lands are now managed by the Palisades Interstate Park Commission whose rules are clearly posted at all entrances.

You have two choices for beginning this hike. For one, park at the principal parking area, 0.2 mile west of the Minnewaska complex road on NY 44. The hike starts along the 2.4-mile access road, which is barred to outside vehicular traffic but used by park managers, so it makes a less than desirable walking route. Use it anyway, unless it is a very hot day, because it is the quickest way to get to the best trails. If it is very hot, a longer, 2.9-mile, much rougher walk starts from the Jenny Lane parking area a half-mile west. This route winds through lush laurel stands and is almost entirely shaded. Note that it takes at least half an hour longer in each direction for this approach. The routes take you to opposite ends of the field where the Scenic Trail begins.

As you start along the access road, variously called Lower Awosting Road or Peter's Kill Road, for the lovely stream that you hear below and to your left, you will see several paths that could take you to its shaded valley. A stiff pace of forty-five minutes brings you to the open field with comfort stations to the right as you enter the field.

A huge pine tree in the middle of the field sports the turquoise blazes of the Long Path that you will be following. These turquoise blazes gradually are replacing the old yellow ones that previously marked this section of the Scenic Trail. Turn left, across a sort of causeway, on the road that leads to Lake Awosting. Immediately across the causeway there is a left fork to the Scenic Trail.

The route, occasionally marked with cairns, leads up over open ledges and is not always obvious as it zigzags uphill. You cross a stream and pause to look back at a wonderful panorama of the distant Catskills. The path turns to follow a ledge covered with hemlock and laurel, high above a deep ravine on your right. You pass one more pretty overlook that is just off the trail, then start to descend, steeply, into Huntington Ravine, a deep hemlock-filled valley with a small stream.

The path through the ravine leads you up to an overhanging ledge and Rainbow Falls, a small cascade that in spring shoots out over the horizontally faulted cliff.

Below the falls, the path leads down across the stream, then left and up the far side of the ravine. You turn to climb gently out of the valley, then up to Upper Awosting Lake Road. Turn right on it for one of the most beautiful parts of the walk. Those handsomely built old carriage roads are so comfortable for walking, and this one is bordered by the tall, sheltering Litchfield Ledge.

In ten minutes, you will turn left on a narrow path and begin to climb, then scramble, over ledges through viburnum thickets. There are spectacular views back across the ravine to the Catskills and west to Lake Awosting. As you wind along on open ledges, you catch sight of Castle Point toward which you are headed. You briefly leave the escarpment to intersect a road from Lake Awosting. You could shorten the trip by turning right here toward the lake, but go left instead, curving up around a hairpin turn of Battlement Terrace and out to Castle Point. Somehow, it is possible to spend an hour and forty minutes on the walk past Rainbow Falls and along the ledges, a distance from the field of not much more than a mile and a half. On a good day, you will have many lovely impressions to justify the slow pace.

(Note: The USGS map and some previous maps do not show correctly the deep hairpin turn of the Kempton Ledge and Castle Point Carriage Road. You could follow it down to its intersection with the Hamilton Point Road and avoid the scramble that the Scenic Trail now follows.)

While you are contemplating the views from Castle Point overlook, ponder on

View from Castle Point on the Scenic Trail

the ledges down which the arrows direct
your continuing route. Rock climbing is
not for the faint of heart, and while this
climb may not be technical, it can be a
scary scramble, with the leaf-strewn path
at the bottom providing still more slippery
footing.

When you meet the Lower Carriage
Road (the Hamilton Point and Palmaghatt
Road), turn right for just over a hundred
yards. Just opposite the point where the
Castle Point Road joins the Hamilton
Point Road, turn left on the path toward
Margaret Cliff.

The varied and ingeniously designed
Scenic Trail continues down through a

cleft between huge boulders and right into a mossy, wet cave that looks for a moment like the end of the line. An arrow left leads through a chute—someone's idea of fun—then out to a rough walk on the conglomerate rock. (Actually, the cave and chute are the work of Maurice Avery, who designed the trail and for a time worked to maintain it.) The trail here is just below the edge of the scarp. There is a small stream to ford in a sylvan dell, then you are out on a carriage road again, this one called Slate Bank Road.

Here you merely cross the road and head back into the woods, turning to climb another ledge. You finish the scramble with an oh-wow view back to the two ledges below Castle Point as well as those below Hamilton Point. Margaret Cliff is a choice spot.

The trail continues along the ridge line through scrubby growth with occasional glimpses of Lake Awosting and the Catskills. You intersect a carriage road again, this one called Spruce Glen Drive; the time for the three-quarter mile between the carriage roads is about thirty minutes.

Follow Spruce Glen Drive north for no more than a hundred yards to a sharp left turn back and up toward Murray Hill. Twenty minutes more of following the cliff edge, and your trail again intersects a carriage road. You will walk along it, past the last clifftop view, which is Murray Hill, and follow it as it turns north for less than half a mile, or a ten-minute walk to the lake shore. The three-quarter-mile segment around Murray Hill requires a bit over half an hour.

At the lakeshore, turn right and in a very few minutes you reach a lovely point—the perfect rest stop. Lake Awosting, at 1,800 feet in elevation, is a true glacial lake, lying in a trough below the cliffs, as are the others in the chain of lakes that descends from the southwest following the dip of the range.

Your route back is the carriage road along the lakeshore with but one fork. At the fork, turn left, continuing north around the end of the lake. The walk along the lakeshore is as pleasant as any part of your day. At the head of the lake, stay left at the intersection with Upper Awosting Lake Road, then, across the outlet, turn right and you will return quickly to the field you left to head for Litchfield Ledge. Estimate an hour and a quarter for the less than two-mile walk along the lake and back to the field.

The Scenic Trail is such a delight that you must be certain to allow adequate time to enjoy all six miles of ledges, views, and quiet spots. The five-mile round-trip walk to its beginning does make it a long day, but a great one.

20

Ice Caves and Napanoch Point

Distance: 7.5 miles
Time: 6 hours or more depending on time spent
    exploring the Ice Caves
Vertical rise: 1,800 feet
Maps: USGS 7½' Ellenville; USGS 7½' Napanoch; NY–NJTC
    Shawangunk Trails, #9

There are two ways to approach the Ice Caves of the Shawangunks. Parking can be a problem at one entrance, so this hike is designed to minimize that problem and provide a loop walk with additional destinations that sample other features of the western ridges of the range. The hike starts in Ellenville. From Canal Street near the center of town head east on Berme Road, and drive past the landfill to a ballfield. Park nearby and walk east uphill until you meet Smiley Road, an eroded dirt track at the edge of the forested slopes. **CAUTION:** *The trail from Smiley Road to Napanoch Point is open to the public. However, the part of the hike to High Point and Ice Caves may be closed in the future, or permission and fees may be required.*

Turn left, northeast, and follow Smiley Road as it heads gradually uphill, with one switchback south shortly after the beginning. The roadway zigzags gradually uphill through tall forests, quite a change from the eastern slopes. It was a real feat to build this road into the side of the hill — you can marvel at its construction as you climb gently toward Shingle Gully. That stream crossing looks to be directly downhill from the Ice Caves where the caves are shown erroneously

on most maps — including the USGS one. The new NY–NJTC maps and the map accompanying this hike are correct.

The roadway becomes a shingle-filled gully with only occasional views to break up the trek. The coarser rock beneath your feet differs from the eastern slopes you traverse in the other hikes in the Gunks. This Shawangunk grit was quarried to create millstones for the first settlers in the Rondout Valley, which lies to the west of the range.

At 2.3 miles, after an hour of walking, you cross a crystal-clear stream and enter a hemlock-covered area. Fifteen minutes later, at 2.6 miles, you pass a woods road forking right. A second stream crossing follows, and within fifteen minutes a second road forks right. You will take it after you visit Napanoch Point. Continuing on the carriage road for less than ten minutes, you see a sign painted on a stone, directing you left to a promontory that lies about a hundred yards from the roadway. Some people think the true Napanoch Point is the lower extension of this promontory, a point that overhangs Napanoch settlement.

Your walks on the Shawangunks cannot fail to interest you in the region's special flora, a transition between the northern boreal forests of the Catskill high peaks and the southern forests distinguished by oaks, hickory, and pitch pine. Patches of laurel and azaleas, blooming in May, dot the range. And, on every open spot, blueberries abound. At one time blueberries were harvested commercially, and often the slopes were burned to promote the bushes' growth.

Napanoch Point, at 3.3 miles, is a good place for lunch. From it, you retrace your steps to the first roadway and turn left on it through a deep hemlock glen beside a stream. Shortly beyond, beaver have managed to flood the roadway, and a detour around to the left may be necessary. Sometime after you pass the new beaver pond, as you begin to climb, look back to enjoy views of the Catskills. Within a fifty-minute walk, 1.2 miles from Napanoch Point, the fire tower on High Point looms above you.

From this promontory, the view of Rondout Valley is most impressive, backed as it is by the mountains of the southern Catskills where the Long Trail

crosses Peekamoose and Table from the Rondout Valley. The high peaks are easily identified with the steep slopes of Wittenberg hiding Cornell, with Slide behind. The Devil's Path Mountains are north or north-northwest of you, with Plateau, Sugar Loaf, Twin, and Indian Head running easterly out of Stony Clove through Mink Hollow. Stony Clove is the deep U-shaped valley; Pecoy Notch and Jimmy Dolan's Notch also are visible.

In the southwest part of the clearing that lies below the tower you will find a red-marked trail. It heads down a slope through the strangest terrain of trees stunted so that you look right over their tops. Gnarled trees intersperse the bare rock openings, sites that are, here in the Shawangunks, often inhabited by rattlesnakes. At times this section of trail can be wet underfoot. And, if you venture off the trail to find dry footing, you will run smack into dense thickets of laurel; now, perhaps, you can understand the feelings of John F. Stokes, the man who originally owned the land that later became Mohonk. He protested that "I suppose . . .

the creator made everything for some-one; but what in the world he ever made that pizen laurel for I can't see. It never grows big enough for firewood and the cattle won't eat it." Yet people travel great distances to see its bloom. Those who do not stop to appreciate the beauty of the laurel and all the other plants as well as the Shawangunk birds are missing much the range has to offer.

After a thirty-minute gradual descent of about 1.2 miles, you reach the point just below the brow of the hill where it begins to drop off more steeply. Here, you will see paths heading right. Be careful, but do follow them. They lead to the edge of the ravines with the Ice Caves. You can follow the crevices downhill until you gain entry to the ravine, or you can follow the crevices as they curve uphill to the north-east. The caves were formed as a whole piece of the mountain pulled away, creat-ing a semicircular ravine, whose major

Late afternoon sun highlights the entrance to the Ice Caves

crevice—the grand canyon of the Shawangunks—is hundreds of feet across and a hundred feet deep. South of the crevice are many minor fissures. The northern end of the canyon curves around reaching close to the top of Shin-gle Gully. There are many places to ex-plore; and with the early afternoon sun filtering in, photographs are possible. For some of the deeper crevices, take a flashlight. Ice persists in some places well into summer, so caution is advised. For some, a rope is helpful.

Allow plenty of time to explore the caves. For your descent, return to the red trail, which becomes a narrow woods path as it winds gently down in a just-over-thirty-minute, mile-long walk to a road. The limited parking along this pri-vate road makes this approach to the Ice Caves undesirable. The road s-curves down to a small park beside North Gully stream. From here it is less than a twenty-minute 0.8 mile walk through town to your car.

21

Mohonk

Distance: Approximately 7 miles
Time: 6 hours
Vertical rise: Many short climbs, none more than 200 feet
Maps: USGS 7½' Mohonk Lake; NY–NJTC Shawangunk
   Trails, #10 & #10A; park map

How about a hike that has as much fun as a trip to a county fair? The equivalent of roller coasters, snap the whip, a merry-go-round, and intriguing tent shows beckons at Mohonk.

Mohonk Preserve is the gem of the Shawangunks. The Mohonk Mountain House, a private hotel surrounded by the Preserve, reflects the leisure and elegance of old-time vacations. The trails and walks that circle round the hotel were laid out with the same nineteenth-century attitude that fostered the hotel. Today they are a marvel of rock climbs, lover's lanes, deep woods walks, and vantage points that reflect their builders' humor. Every spot is named, every path has been walked many times before, but the fun and sense of discovery are still there. For a modest fee, you can walk the Preserve's trails just as Victorian vacationers did a century ago.

The Shawangunks owe their development to the vision of Alfred H. Smiley, who first saw the escarpment in 1869. Alfred later developed the Minnewaska resort. His twin brother, Albert K., purchased the first 280 acres for $28,000 and began the development of the hotel and grounds. At Albert's death in 1912, the property had grown through over a hundred purchases to encompass 5,000 acres. The brothers transformed a "labyrinth of boulders" unfolded into "two fertile valleys with the Catskill range against the western sky" into a premier resort designed "to make accessible the beauty and romance of the mountain. The systematic construction of paths began. Through labyrinth and forest, over ravines and under precipices, through fissures and solemn vales, year after year the trails were made and then widened into walks."

The visitors' parking area at Mohonk is on Mountain Rest Road west of New Paltz. Here you pay a five-dollar entrance fee that entitles you to park and walk everywhere but in the restricted central area of the Mohonk Mountain House. You will receive a map, and for another dollar you can ride a bus to the visitors' center, open daily in the summer and on weekends in winter for skiing.

You could not possibly walk all the trails, even on a weekend; the guide says there are 128 miles of paths and carriage roads. But, it is possible to sample some of the best and whet your appetite for a return visit to sample more.

On the trail in Mohonk Preserve

Let's start out by following the signs to the Lake Side Path and turn south away from the lodge to Labyrinth Path. A sign warning of "crevices and scrambles which require hiking over and under huge rocks" greets you. You are advised to wear sneakers or nonslip shoes and to carry no hand-held articles. The warning continues that the crevice just below Sky Top is deep and narrow, and its ladders and scramble are not for everyone.

And so the fantasy atmosphere of Mohonk's walks begins. You cannot help but wonder at the women in long skirts who flirtatiously clambered through the passages in tumbled rock slabs, with chutes and ladders. Sometimes you are buried deep within the cliffs that seem to peel away from the mountainside, sometimes you emerge to glimpse the hotel across the lake. Arrows point the way, and within twenty minutes you see an intersection where a left fork leads to Sky Top Road. If you are still game, continue straight ahead—the best is yet to come. Red arrows and rectangles point the way over an open rock scramble with views across to the cliffs on the far side of the lake, topped with precariously perched gazebos, and overall, a view toward the Catskills.

Near the end of the scramble, arrows point up to the crevice, which narrows to no more than eighteen inches wide and is some twenty feet deep, with a climb over rocks and up ladders that totals thirty feet in height. After you have finished this, laughing and groaning, you have begun to savor Mohonk's adult playground.

A sign points to the Pinnacle Path, and another ladder and scramble bring you out on Sky Top Road heading up to the Albert K. Smiley memorial stone tower with its superb views. It takes about an hour for the less-than-one-mile walk from the visitors' center to Sky Top via the Labyrinth. You may surmise that directions here are superfluous, but follow on, to sample Mohonk's best.

Briefly head down the road and turn left, away from the crevice route, onto Pinnacle Path, which turns sharply down at the first overhanging, rustic seat. This precipitous clifftop walk leads you to a fork; take the left turn, down, and follow signs to Pinnacle Rock, a photogenic column separated from the cliff.

Turn uphill, following the Mohonk Path, crossing carriage roads as you climb. Shortly after your narrow path begins to descend steeply, you reach Reservoir Road and turn left beneath overhanging ledges and deep shade. The soft moss base of these old carriage roads makes beautiful walking.

When you reach Sky Top Road, head toward the hotel to circle round to its northern side. Notice the Museum, which you will want to visit another day. About forty minutes suffices for this one-mile segment of the walk.

Turn onto Eagle Cliff Road with signs pointing toward the Granary and Undercliff. Turn left on Lambdin's Path, where you will walk down and under a bridge to Undercliff Path. Here, turn right, away from the hotel. Stop at one of the gazebos for a brief rest, then continue to the end of the lake and turn away from Undercliff on a faint path through a draw that quickly intersects lovely Woodland Road. Here turn right toward Humpty Dumpty and Cope's Point.

You emerge from the deep shade of tall trees to a gazebo with a gorgeous view of the Trapps. Turn here toward Humpty Dumpty and the Plateau Path. From hopping on sun-warmed rocks you descend into a deep cool glen with bursts of moist air telling of deeper crevices beneath. Look back at intervals, for at a point you will see an exquisitely framed view of the Trapps. Follow the deep cleft into a hemlock ravine where lots of scrambling will take you to a fork.

Try the blue blazes that continue down—a nearly straight drop—to Giant's Workshop. You begin to feel a bit silly, like a child in a magical kingdom.

You have traversed so many paths and found such a variety of routes that it is hard to believe it is less than three-quarters of an hour since you left the lake. The path emerges on Minnewaska Road, and turning right, uphill, you shortly intersect Laurel Path Road, my idea of the perfect woodland road. Your map shows that at any point you could continue on the old carriage roads back to the visitors' center. But, to continue the adventure, turn right on Plateau Path, then turn again onto blue-marked Cathe-dral Path. The way straight, marked with red, circles back to the Giant's Workshop and the trail you have already followed. Cathedral Path will lead you up through a jumble of rocks—doesn't one look like a huge whale?—you may catch the "naming fever" that infected the trails' creators. A red trail joins from the right, you go leftish and up beneath the cliff, then up it to emerge on a rock ledge with a gazebo and views. If that spot is occupied, turn left on Copes Lookout Road.

Beyond the next charming overlook, turn right from Copes Lookout Road to Copes Lookout Path, which quickly brings you back to the Eaglecliff Road near the tennis courts. You will easily

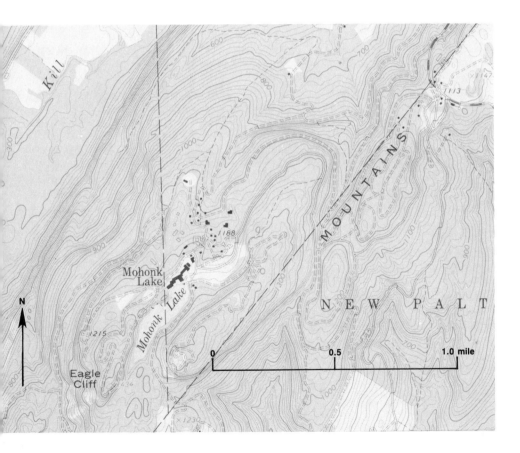

spend two hours savoring these two miles of walks and scrambles. Have you noticed how close the carriage roads and paths are, yet how separated they seem because they circle the mountain at such varied elevations?

A right on Eaglecliff Road gives you a beautiful walk beneath hemlocks and ledges, again in the deep, cool shade. Pause again for the views from Artists' Rock, then turn again downhill. Instead of following the carriage road, look for the red arrow-marked path that weaves between switchbacks on the carriage road and keeps you close to clifftop as you descend. Look across the lake to the crevice below Sky Top that you climbed earlier in the day. The Sky Top loop on Eaglecliff Road and back to the visitors' center is about 1.8 miles and takes one-and-a-quarter hours.

You return to the visitors' center, and look for the arrows to Mossy Brook Road and signs pointing to the shortest way to the parking area, 1.5 miles and a forty-minute walk. The route takes you past impressive views of the Hudson Valley and again onto a woodland path, this time through an exquisite valley. It leads you up Whitney Road to Huguenot Drive and a short stretch along that road back to the parking area.

Eastern
Catskills

Mill ruins at Vernooy Kill Falls

Vernooy Kill Falls

Distance: 3.6 miles
Time: 2 hours
Vertical rise: 640 feet
Map: USGS 7½′ Kerhonkson

Vernooy Kill Falls is the site of an old gristmill now surrounded by farmlands. A walk to the falls is short and delightful and a time to think about farmers of long ago.

The route to the trailhead passes through farmlands that are giving way to resorts or forest cover. From the intersection of NY 44 and 55 with NY 209, go north 1.2 miles on NY 209 to the traffic light in Kerhonkson. Turn left here on Clay Hill Road, which is unmarked. You reach a stop at 2.5 miles where Pataukunk Road, also designated County

Route 3, comes in from the right. Turn left on County Route 3 and then turn left again in 0.2 mile on Cherrytown Road. Again there are no signs to guide you, but there are beautiful vistas back to the Shawangunks.

Cherrytown road winds west and then north. You will be reassured that you are following the correct route by the blue paint slashes that mark this stretch of road as a portion of the Long Path. You pass Baker Road 3.65 miles from County Route 3, 6.3 miles from Kerhonkson. Immediately, Upper Cherrytown Road

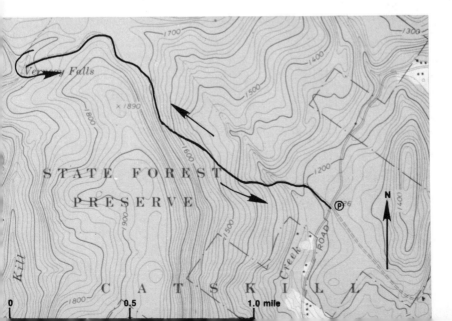

crosses a brook, and just beyond it, before the road crosses over Mombaccus Creek, you turn left again, this time onto Upper Cherrytown Road. Follow it north for 3.15 miles to the trailhead which is on the west, left, side of the road, with a parking area on the right.

The trail, a portion of the Long Path, is marked with blue DEC hiking disks. It follows an old town road through a lovely laurel stand across a little stream with a rock-hop crossing. Two hundred yards farther you will cross Mombaccus Creek on a snowmobile bridge to the right of the roadway and briefly follow the creek uphill. The road makes a sweeping S-curve as it begins to climb the ridge, rising out of the valley's deep hemlock stands into second growth hardwoods. The uphill route is steady, gradually leaving laurel behind. You pass through an area of blowdowns, then, as the trail levels out to round the hillside, you may notice a road that forks left. You continue on the obvious route, shortly hearing the falls and beginning a small descent to Vernooy Kill.

The spot is charming, with a bridge across the stream from which you can view the falls. Below, one solid wall of the ruins of the mill extends along the eastern shore, and other rock walls delineate the channel through which water was diverted to power the mill. You can try to discover the way water was used to power the mill or extend your visit in a number of other ways. The hemlock bank to the southeast of the falls is an attractive place to picnic or camp, though it can be crowded on summer weekends. You can walk downstream along the western shore to a lovely picnic spot and more foundations. Below the mill site, Vernooy Kill continues to tumble over boulders, creating cascades and small falls in the secluded valley. There is a short path along the western shore to lead you briefly downstream. You can continue the walk west on the snowmobile trail through a spruce and hemlock swamp with a lovely understory of *Lycopodia* and ferns. A faint path leads north along the stream to other smaller falls and pools. The Long Path continues north along an old road. Wherever you turn, you can explore the foundations of houses and barns and follow old stone fences. And, you can wonder, as I did, about the origins of the mill. The Kill was named for Cornelius Vernooy, one of the very first settlers in the Rondout Valley. In the early 1700s, he brought the area's first gristmill to Warwarsing, with machinery imported from Holland. But the name of the settlers upstream at the falls remains a mystery.

Peekamoose and Table

Distance: 8.5 miles (from Denning Trailhead)
Time: 5 hours
Vertical rise: 1,750 feet
Map: NY–NJTC Catskill Trails Map #43

What will impress you most about Peekamoose and its environs is the remarkable clarity and storybook forests of the Rondout Creek and its valley. The Rondout is conceived on the south- and east-facing slopes of Rocky, Lone, and Peekamoose Mountains, and is joined by the malachite waters of Peekamoose Lake as it swells through Bull Run and joins its east branch at Sundown. John Burroughs loved this flashy, pellucid brook, vowing that "If I were a trout I should ascend every stream till I found the Rondout."

While you can make this hike as a back-the-way-you-came jaunt, bagging both Table and Peekamoose in what would amount to a moderate nine-mile, 1800-foot ascent from Denning, you also can leave one vehicle at the Denning Trailhead and another at the Long Path (blue) trail directly to Peekamoose, on Peekamoose Road just east of Bull Run. Or make it an overnighter, camping among the intricate islands and peninsulas created by the confluence of Deer Shanty Brook, Donovan Brook, and the upper reaches of the Neversink's East Branch. This popular spot with its lean-to and untold campsites upstream along the Neversink is certainly as close to heaven

as anyone can be—and still be in the Catskills.

Whatever you choose, be warned of the approach directly to Peekamoose Mountain from the south, along the Peekamoose Road above Bull Run. This trail has long been a model of demoralizing ascents, with its 2,643-foot elevation gain within 3.5 miles. The Denning Trail (Phoenicia–East Branch Trail) with its crossing at Deer Shanty Brook is the more gentle and scenic option, and it will save you 1000 feet of elevation. If you wish only to climb Peekamoose (which doesn't have Table's view), are rushed for time, in top condition, and up to an unrelenting, difficult ascent, the Long Path access is the shortest route.

If you choose the yellow Phoenicia–East Branch Trail (PE), start at Denning. From Big Indian, west of Phoenicia, travel south on County Route 47 through Oliverea, Winnisook, and Frost Valley, and turn left in Claryville onto County Route 19 (Denning Road). Follow this straight into Denning to the trailhead parking area, a total distance from Big Indian of some thirty miles. A more complicated route is from Boiceville on NY 28A south to West Shokan, turning right on County Route 42 (Peekamoose Road), passing the strenuous blue trail (and Long Path) access ten miles from West Shokan. Then bear right into Grahamsville, Unionville, and Curry on NY 55, turning right at Curry to Claryville, and again right into Denning and to the trailhead, also a total of thirty miles.

Park at the road's end where trail signs to Slide Mountain and the Denning lean-to are posted. The setting is a high farming valley plain studded by large mansions and the summer retreats of the wealthy and reclusive. You may see deer feeding close to the road here. Once we even rolled apples from roadside trees to waiting deer, who munched them happily.

Follow the trail through a hemlock woods over a crude road, crossing two small plank bridges and a small seasonal brook. Within twenty-five minutes you will reach a trail junction, where you turn right toward the Denning lean-to. Go downhill into a wet area (seasonal), keep-

ing an eye on the markers (blue), and continuing steeply down across two streams, one of which could be a dry bed at various times of year. The trail is better marked beyond these, and it will bring you to the lean-to within a few minutes.

There are many campsites upstream from the lean-to, perhaps hundreds, with several campfire rings constructed along the creek's edge. These primitive sites continue seemingly without end, along the banks of both Deer Shanty Brook and the Neversink. The "bridges" spanning these creeks are single logs, hewn flat on the walking surface, so watch your step or rock-hop it. The blue markers and Long Path blazes are good as the trail leaves opposite the lean-to.

Go uphill through a lush forest of fern, oxalis, club moss, and huge birch. Within

a half-hour the trail will level somewhat, skirting a ridge exposing Woodhull and Van Wyck Mountains to the southwest. The trail will rise and fall for a while as you go through thin stands of hardwood, climbing through broken rock ledges and taking frequent breaks. Within forty-five minutes of leaving the lean-to you reach a ledge among the cherry trees with a view of Peekamoose and to the south. Several more spur trails lead to the right twenty or thirty feet off the trail, some with worthwhile views. Beware—these are dangerous ledges. Through the trees to the left (north) as you continue, you may see Slide and its neighboring peaks, and, as you gain in elevation, you'll identify Panther, parts of Giant Ledge, Lone, Rocky, Balsam Cap, and Friday.

Within two hours of the Denning lean-to you will reach Table's summit. There is no view here—only a canister belonging to the Catskill 3500 Club. The best view of the entire trip awaits. Continue through thick spruce and fir until you reach a sign (painted in blue at this time) saying "VIEW" and indicating a spur trail, to the left, or east of the main trail. Within five minutes you will reach a rock outcropping. Slide is the long ridge close in front of you to the north. To the right you see Lone, Wittenberg and Cornell, Friday, Rocky, Balsam Cap, Hanover, the Ashokan Reservoir, West Kill and Hunter between Slide and Cornell, the Blackheads, Plateau, and Sugar Loaf. Through Pecoy Notch you can see Kaaterskill High Peak. This is nearly the entire Devil's Path skyline.

When and if you've had enough of this rare sight, continue on the main trail to Peekamoose, which you can see before you as you descend. Some faraway views are available along this downhill section of trail—extending beyond the Gunks and into the Highlands. Even Anthony's Nose and the deep gulch spanned by the Bear Mountain Bridge can be seen with binoculars, or good eyes.

As you drop into the fragrant, coniferous saddle between Table and Peekamoose, the trail becomes wet, and within ten minutes you'll begin climbing again. You may see a vague Y in the trail as you approach the summit of Peekamoose. Go right, reaching the summit where a large boulder sits in a small clearing, surrounded by scrub evergreens. This boulder can be climbed for more views—but they are inferior to Table's. (There is no canister.)

If you are walking out to Peekamoose Road instead of returning, continue ahead following steeply downhill through a series of ledges and overlooks, following the backbone of a long ridge extending south-southwest. Within a half-hour of leaving the summit, following frequent Long Path (blue) blazes and trail markers (blue), you will reach an outstanding viewpoint exposing the Rondout, Neversink and Mongaup Valleys, Samson Mountain, Bangle Hill, Breath Hill, Little Rocky, and some interesting ridges to the west. Avoid the dotted trail, which leaves this point east of Buttermilk Falls Brook; it crosses private lands. From this point you will be walking down, through a dense, predominantly ash and maple forest with a beech understory. The trail continues amid white violets, huge cottonwoods, and red and white pines as you gradually go downhill, meeting up with a skid or fire road that becomes steadily eroded and finally reaches Peekamoose Road, two hours' walking time from the summit. If you choose this way out, you'll be glad you avoided it on the way in.

Ashokan High Point

Distance: 7.5 miles
Time: 5½ hours
Vertical rise: 1,980 feet
Map: NY–NJTC Catskill Trails Map #43

This fine hike is not included in contemporary guidebooks. The trail is not marked, there are no signs indicating the mountain's presence, and there are few people who know about the outstanding scenery it affords. In truth, it is one of the most attractive trails and biggest scenic payoffs in the Catskill Range.

The trail to Ashokan High Point's summit is an old settlement road that has been so well built that it requires little maintenance. The surface is hard-packed dirt and gravel, where few seedlings will hold. It has been so well drained in past years that erosion has caused little damage. Old stone walls and ditch construction protect it from the advancing forest. Only the overhanging boughs that occasionally you will duck under betray any need for trail maintenance, much of which is done by a few loyal hikers and the Boy Scouts. Because it is so little known, the trail also is quite clean. All things considered—it is a rare find in an era earmarked by overuse and exploitation.

The trail to High Point shows on the NY–NJTC map as a dotted line, keyed as an unmarked trail. The map is accurate to a point. It shows the correct route to the summit, but omits some side

trails that might cause confusion. It also indicates a spur running from the summit and east to a lower summit (at 2800 feet) that no longer exists. Don't let the lack of marking deter you, however. The moderate-difficulty trail is self-guiding in its entirety, and it is hard to get lost if you pay attention to the map and text.

Find the trailhead by turning south on NY 28A from NY 28 in Boiceville west of Kingston. Follow 28A for three miles to West Shokan. Here, Peekamoose Road (County Route 42) runs uphill along the Bush Kill. After 3.9 miles, you will see on the left a dirt path barricaded by a steel cable with, as of this writing, a fifty-five-gallon drum suspended from it. Park along the road. State land and Forest Preserve signs are posted nearby. As you climb under the cable you'll notice a small timber bridge crossing Kanape Brook that leads to the trail, or jeep road.

Follow the trail uphill through a typical Catskill slope forest of beech, birch, and maple, slowly climbing up and away from Kanape Brook, which is on your right. Within ten minutes you will cross one of several stone culverts that run under the trail, draining the northwest watershed of the mountain. These are structures you ordinarily won't see on Catskill trails. Several are completely handmade, the ditch itself lined with bluestone drywalls and capped with larger flat stones that you will walk over. You will begin to see some very attractive bluestone drywalls (not mortared) along this part of the trail, as well as some stone bridges that span seasonal creeks. You'll cross two such bridges and climb gradually but steadily into an area where mountain laurel appears.

Within five or ten minutes you will reach a Y in the trail, on which you bear right, staying on the more-established trail. Shortly afterward, you pass a small spring on the left that has been dug by hand and built up with stone. In another ten minutes the trail crosses Kanape Brook into a clearing with a bench and a mortared brick and stone fireplace. This is a pretty spot—the brook forms a larger pool as it flows from the shaded conifer forest upstream. Balsam fir now appear,

and shortly afterward some larger hemlocks. There are many attractive camping sites all along this trail, particularly through this section.

Keep going uphill, never strenuously, for another twenty minutes through a second-growth forest. You will curve gradually toward the east and suddenly reach higher, open forest where the trail turns grassy amid the oak and laurel. You may notice a good trail branching to the right at this point. Keep going, until within five minutes you reach a T where you are in an airy, forested saddle between High Point and Mombaccus Mountains at 2000 feet. There is a campfire ring here and several flat camping areas.

Turn left (northeast) here for the one-mile, 1000-foot elevation gain to the summit. Pass a road that goes off to your left

The Devil's Path from Ashokan High Point

slightly beyond the trail intersection, and follow straight ahead, beginning to climb uphill in a moment. In five minutes you will pass a vague footpath to the trail's right. Continue uphill into a slide and ledge area over broken rock footing. Views will appear as you climb through this red oak, maple, and blueberry cover on your way through terracing terrain. From saddle to summit takes not more than forty-five minutes.

The summit is a small rock ledge with an east-to-southwest exposure, revealing the edge of the Ashokan Reservoir, the Kingston–Rhinecliff Bridge, the Shawangunks from Mohonk to Minnewaska and down to Sams Point, and beyond into the Hudson Highlands. Carvings from 1878 show in the summit stones, along with several anchor bolts from an early observation tower. North of the summit several trails wander into the woods, one of which leads a hundred yards to an open westerly overlook with good views of Slide, Friday, Balsam Cap, Rocky, Lone, Table, and Peekamoose. This short side trip is a must!

Ashokan summit has a fine collection of views to pick from, but what will astonish you most is its blueberries, which are everywhere and rank easily as the best of the Catskill patches. The thick bushes cover the entire unshaded summit, and the unusually large berries remain seemingly unnoticed until harvested by frost.

Although it may not seem possible as you stand on Ashokan High Point's true summit, the views (and the blueberries) are better on the low knob you can see just east of you. This is a short bushwhack, some of it on an obscure and for the most part indistinguishable foot trail. Even without a compass it is difficult to get lost, but it is a good idea for beginning bushwhackers to have one along just in case. This quarter-mile trip to the eastern summit is so worthwhile that it should not be missed.

To get there, drop down around the summit's north side on a vague footpath that will disappear eventually, sometimes to re-emerge looking like a well-trodden deer path. Follow east (a compass bearing would be accurate at 125° with declination figured in) and into a saddle with long rock ledges running north to south. The terrain will undulate gently afterward, gradually ascending to bring you out to the open easterly expanse. Figure on about fifteen minutes for this bushwhack.

Here you will see many ledges and rock overhangs where you can search for more views, but the terrain is easy. In autumn it is a montage of burgundy berry bushes that grow thickly and reach to knee height. Scrub oak turns the color of brickdust on amber. You can see almost the entire Ashokan, a long flat strip of indigo among the valley's greenness, where colors will change in weeks to come. Spun into the scene are the somber, drab outcroppings of rock that pockmark the summits and ranges beyond, and the short stilts of battered, nutbrown tree trunks, festooned with the scarlet berry clusters of mountain ash.

Looking left (north) from east to west you observe Overlook, Plattekill, Indian Head, Jimmy Dolan Notch, Twin, Pecoy Notch, Sugar Loaf, Mink Hollow, Plateau, Stony Clove Notch, Hunter, Diamond Notch, and West Kill Mountain. To the north are Wittenberg and Cornell. To the east and beyond the reservoir are the Taconics and the Berkshires. Moving westward is the long Shawangunk Ridge and the flat plain of the Neversink, Rondout, and Mongaup Rivers. Suddenly Mombaccus again fills your eye, and you've covered about 270 degrees, for what promises to be one of the best overlooks in the Catskill Mountains.

You will also be able to see the roads around the Ashokan Reservoir (New York City's water supply), which provide outstanding views of the range. The hike out from the knob and back over Ashokan High Point will take you about two hours. Avoid the shorter southerly access, for it is private.

If you have time now, you might want to drive across the dam and causeway on a longer route back to NY 28. Instead of going left when you get to the bottom of Peekamoose Road in West Shokan, go right and stay on 28A until you reach a left turn (approximately six miles) that you will see crosses the reservoir, providing views of Ashokan High Point and the Catskill High Peaks.

This huge impoundment has an unsettling history. Its construction required the relocation of seven towns, eleven miles of railroad, sixty-four miles of roads, and the valley's 2000 inhabitants. 2600 coffins in thirty-two cemeteries were exhumed and moved, dumps were dug up and disinfected, buildings were burned and sanitized, and recompenses made. It took twenty-five years to settle all the claims involved.

If the water table is high you will want to see the spillway, which you can reach by staying on NY 28A (east) toward Kingston. This is where wastewater from the lower basin finds its way to the Hudson River via the Esopus Creek.

Ashokan meant *place to fish* to the Iroquois, as it does to modern fishermen who regularly catch trout weighing up to twenty pounds below the weir. The Ashokan is the wintering place for trout that spawn upstream in the Esopus, a fact that has made the stream famous for its annual spring run, particularly of the rainbow trout.

Mount Tremper

Distance: 4.3 miles
Time: 4 hours
Vertical rise: 1,960 feet
Map: NY–NJTC Catskill Trails Map #41

The trail to Mount Tremper is most direct and interesting from the southwest access along old NY 28, or the Old Plank Road, south of Phoenicia. It is also accessible from Willow, off NY 212, on the longer, blue-marked trail from Jessup Road.

Both trails form a section of the Long Path as it approaches the Devil's Path from the south through Mink Hollow. Switchbacks characterize the red trail to Mount Tremper, transforming this otherwise difficult 2,000-foot ascent into a moderate hike. The path zigzags across the slope, turning at convenient points of terrain to double back on itself, sometimes nearly 180 degrees. Long before hiking became fashionable, the road was used for log hauling and stone quarrying, and later for fire control and maintenance.

The red trail begins on the east side of the Esopus Creek, off County Route 40 (Old Plank Road or old NY 28), 2.3 miles northwest of Mount Tremper Corners, or 1.6 miles southeast of Phoenicia. Parking at streamside is ample, and you will most likely be sharing it not with fellow hikers, but with trout fishermen who enjoy the long run of water here known as "sleepy hollow."

You'll be taken with the water's clarity and alpine character. You may see dimpling rises of brown and rainbow trout, whose enduring management has made the creek one of New York State's most valued fisheries. After heavy run-off, though, the Esopus assumes an ugly tinge of mountain grit and remains for days the color of chocolate milk. During these periods, when fishermen are scarce and snow sticks reluctantly in the hemlock shadows, the views from Mount Tremper are at their best.

As you enter the Forest Preserve, don't be deterred by the trail's initial steepness, where logs have been placed to check erosion. It soon levels out, bringing you to the trail register at 0.25 mile. Continue over broken rock and red shale footing, gradually gaining elevation.

Several larger feeder streams intersect the trail, and a culvert appears as you enter a sparse stand of maturing white pine. Evidence of logging is visible in the abundance of thin, second-growth hardwood and several decaying stumps. Yellow paint blazes running north and south-west mark the Forest Preserve boundaries. This piece of trail also sports a few of the Long Path's blue blazes.

As the trail steepens to fifteen or twenty degrees, you cross another culvert, over an energetic brook that cuts a deep gully in the mountainside as it bursts from an uneven-aged hemlock stand. At this point you are twenty minutes into the hike, or almost a half-mile. You will have reached the first switchback when the trail suddenly turns south and uphill, where large maple and ash dominate an understory of young hemlock. To your left (east) and uphill, a long outcropping that has slid in many places starts an interesting visual transition. Water appears from a spring on your left. Fallen rock can be seen below the trail to your right, now heavily covered with moss, the accumulated stuff of ancient forests.

As you come through the next switchback, you'll see a huge pile of quarry tailings, the broken stone that was shoved aside as longer slabs were excavated. It now forms a sort of man-made ridge, covered with thin soil and vegetation. The quarry is accessible from a small, overgrown roadbed on the trail's left that ascends gently into the quarry excavation, which covers an acre or two. Follow it to a high, right-angled rock face, where the slabs were removed. Other than this vertical stone wall, only a small foundation and a few rusted iron remnants bear testimony to the once-thriving industry. During your exploration, beware of the quarry-dwelling rattlesnakes, who habitu-

ally bask in the warm sun of early spring. (They are shy and wary of you.)

Many of the nineteenth century hotel owners disliked the imposing quarries. By the early 1880s Major Jacob H. Tremper's Tremper House was competing for business with the Catskill Mountain House, so could ill afford competition with the nearby bluestone quarries that robbed the hills of their peace and quiet. Alf Evers writes in *The Catskills from Wilderness to Woodstock*, "Boarders grumbled at the ugly quarry scars on mountainsides. They noticed with displeasure a conspicuous quarry erupting even before 1880 near the Catskill Mountain House and a short walk from the romantic Moses Rock, and saw quarry after quarry breaking into other mountain forests. Quarries began to threaten the Tremper House from its flanks, while others were unpleasantly visible. . . . In all parts of the mountains boarders never knew when their surries or tallyhoes might meet a ponderous stone wagon driven by a cursing teamster in the cloud of dust raised by its horses' hoofs and its wheels."*

After you have visited the quarry,

---

*Alf Evers, *The Catskills* (Woodstock, NY: The Overlook Press, 1982), p. 573.

where the dust has long since settled, follow the trail along a flatter section into an oak forest, which turns into the oak and laurel cover typical of higher elevations in the Catskills. At about 1,800 feet above sea level you switchback about 120 degrees on a steepening grade, where paper birch and an occasional white pine appear. You'll have a few glimpses southwest toward southern high peaks during early spring. Once through the switchback, you can look through the trees at northwesterly views toward Sheridan Mountain.

The trail steepens, heading directly uphill, nearly due east. Within a few minutes you see a lean-to on your right. At this point you are 1.6 miles from the trailhead. Keep a sharp eye out for this shelter if you intend to use it, because it's easy to miss, positioned as it is, downhill and facing south. It is in better condition than the summit lean-to, is more private, and has a water source nearby.

Finally, after one more switchback you will climb slightly and walk a long ridge. Just as you expected the summit to appear, you will discover that the ridge continues for another half-mile through a canopy of twisted oak, tormented and battered by exposure. After twenty minutes more hiking, you will reach a stand of bright-barked beech trees on your left, and soon after that the second lean-to.

The fire tower just ahead is closed to the public and its lower staircase has been removed, for its structural integrity is not likely to last. Isolated views are attainable here. The fire tower was built to replace the one on Slide, after the Mount Tremper tract was acquired between 1906 and 1910. Fires occurred on Mount Tremper in 1881, 1888, and again between 1916 and 1917. The area gave heavily of its hemlock stands between 1836 and 1879, with one local tanner recording an all-time harvest of 170,000 cords of bark.

The Tremper House Hotel was built in 1879 near the existing railroad bed at the base of the mountain. It was the Catskill's first railroad hotel, in an era when remoteness was more in fashion, and was visited by so many colorful personalities that it threatened even the popularity of Charles Beach's Catskill Mountain House. Young Oscar Wilde "chose to deliver his aesthetic lectures," according to Evers, "only at the Tremper House and the Kaaterskill Hotel. Wilde praised the Catskills' scenery, but shocked hotel proprietors by stating that their mountain houses are always built in the wrong spots. The top of a mountain is no place for a mountain house . . . it should be put in the valley, there the picturesque and beautiful is ever before you."*

---

*Evers, p. 511.

Overlook Mountain

Distance: 10 miles
Time: 7–9 hours
Vertical rise: 1,250 feet
Map: NY–NJTC Catskill Trails Map #41

The most interesting trail to Overlook Mountain begins at the head of the precipitous Plattekill Clove, reached by the harrowing Platte Clove Mountain Road, which climbs 1,400 feet in two miles. In dry weather, the road is not much of a problem, but it is closed officially during winter months. Portions of the serpentine surface slide into the ravine 500 feet below, and the road is repaired continually. At the guardrails you might want to pull over to spy down at "the wildest and boldest, most picturesque and romantic scenery of the entire Catskills," in the words of H. A. Haring, in his classic *Our Catskill Mountains* (1931).

To find Platte Clove Mountain Road, take NY 212 from its junction with NY 32 in Saugerties, and turn right in Centerville after 2.4 miles, onto Blue Mountain Road. Bear left when you reach a fork at 1.5 miles. Continue straight ahead through the village of West Saugerties and up the mountain road for another 4.5 miles to the trailhead.

You can avoid the steep ascent altogether by coming from the west through Tannersville (on NY 23A), following Spring Street south and Bloomer Road east, which follows into Platte Clove Mountain Road two miles from where

you left NY 23A at Tannersville. From here it is another five miles to the trailhead. Coming from Tannersville avoid the DEC trail signs to Mink Hollow, Twin Mountain, and Devil's Path on Prediger Road. Continue instead to the Catskill Center for Conservation and Development (CCCD) signs, which you will see on the right a mile beyond Prediger Road. Parking is limited here, but there are several spots ahead (southeast on the mountain road).

This is a watershed divide. The northwesterly flowing Schoharie drains Roundtop and Kaaterskill High Peak on the north of its valley and the Devil's Path Mountains (from Indian Head to Hunter) on the south. The Plattekill Creek, flowing east, draws its youthful might from Kaaterskill High Peak, Plattekill Mountain, and Overlook Mountain. From here it flows through the clove to meander sluggishly to the Hudson.

Start your hike by following the green arrows on a white background across Plattekill Creek (tricky during run-off). The trail follows the old Overlook Road, which is washed out and unrecognizable at first, but which soon becomes a pleasant bedrock pathway shadowed in hemlock.

Overlook Mountain

The arrows are intermittent and finally absent but the trail is obvious and soon joins the Devil's Path, marked by red NYSDEC trail markers of the State Forest Wilderness Area. An abandoned quarry apparent to the left just before this junction is easily explored. From late spring on, however, beware of rattlesnakes.

Within another two or three minutes' walking, the red-marked Devil's Path turns right. A series of trail signs mark this junction. Here you proceed straight on a blue-marked trail for the Devil's Kitchen lean-to and eventually Overlook Mountain. New maps show this as marked blue, but markers at this time are inconsistent. Continuing on the blue trail, shortly after this junction, you will discover a vague Y in the trail, on which you bear right, arriving at the Devil's Kitchen lean-to on the Coldkill.

Northeast of the lean-to there is a virgin tract of hemlock and mixed hardwood that has been categorized by the CCCD as a unique plant community. The major ground cover species are alder-leaved viburnum, jack-in-the-pulpit, spinulose wood fern, Canada mayflower, and wood sorrel.

Continuing from the lean-to, on the blue trail, cross over the Coldkill on a wooden bridge, and follow a slight uphill washout until reaching level terrain under oak and laurel cover. To the east you will notice some good views through the oak to the Hudson Valley. About 1.1 miles from where you crossed the Coldkill is Skunk Spring on the right side of the trail. Except for the dry months, this is a great place to slake one's thirst and refill a canteen. The trail now follows an even elevation contour on Plattekill's eastern shoulder at 2,500 feet. On this effortless section of the trail, you will notice the appearance of white birch and get occasional glimpses of the Overlook summit and fire tower to the south.

Three miles into the hike you reach the Echo Lake spur (yellow markers) to your right. This trail drops 500 feet in half a mile to the west. There is a good lean-to at the lake and some attractive camping possibilities, but because of its proximity to a trailhead at Meads, it is an easy hike that allows for overuse by crowds. A rough trail circles Echo Lake, which forms the headwaters of the Sawkill.

The degree of abuse at Echo Lake, at this writing, has been ambitious; the privy has been torn down for firewood and stuffed with litter, the vegetation ravaged, and refuse widely distributed. But it is still worth the trip to see one of the Catskill's few natural lakes and to observe some of the problems the Catskill Forest Preserve faces. You might even try for the echo, which was a favorite pastime of guests from the Overlook Mountain House days.

At the Overlook Mountain and Echo Lake trail junction, you are only 1.9 miles from your destination. Continuing up around the northwest slope of Overlook, there are good views, in the spring, of the Devil's Path mountains. Indian Head (3,573 feet) seems to have appeared from nowhere and is surprisingly close at three miles. Identifying the notches and peaks will be a good lunchtime activity from Overlook's summit.

Within a half hour on this gentle but steady ascent (after passing a good spring), you reach a trail junction near the ruins of the Overlook Mountain House. The trail signs give the wrong distance of 2.5 miles to Devil's Kitchen lean-to; the correct distance is 3.5 miles. Keep in mind, as well, that the stated 5.9 miles to Platte Clove Mountain Road, while accurate if you entered on the red trail from Prediger Road, is actually 4.5 miles for those using the CCCD trail, which you came in on.

Continuing to the east following the blue markers, you will arrive at the summit in another fifteen minutes. The fire tower is still operational and provides one of the few 360-degree views available in the Catskills. (Also on the summit are picnic tables and the small residence for the forest fire observers, one of whom is reported to have placed rattlesnakes in his dresser drawers after having found them rifled by hiking vandals.) Just as inspiring a view is that of Overlook itself from the valley floor, a sight that merited the brushes of Frederic Church and Thomas Cole and prompted the pen of Charles Herbert Moore. The mountain continues to provide inspiration for aspiring artists from the village of Woodstock below.

From the summit, the heavy haze of the Hudson Valley, during most summer days, limits the view east to Kingston and Saugerties and to the Hudson itself. On the marvelous clear days of spring, autumn, and winter, though, you can see into Connecticut and Massachusetts. The Hudson Highlands to the southeast can be seen too if the air is very clear.

In 1871, the Overlook Mountain House opened here, but despite its various distinctions it was not a great success. It burned completely in 1875, was reconstructed in 1878, and burned again in 1924. In 1928, under new ownership, the existing poured concrete foundation and walls, near the old hotel site, were started. Walls, windows, and plumbing were about all that was completed when the crash of 1929 happened, when the project was abandoned.

If you want to hike to the summit of Overlook from Meads, the trailhead begins at the road's height on Meads

© 1983 New York–New Jersey Trail Conference

Mountain, 2.5 miles north of the Woodstock village green. There is good parking space opposite the Zen Buddhist monastery, and the walk is an easy uphill hike of two miles following the red markers.

The Old Mountain Road to Palenville Overlook

Distance: 8 miles
Time: 5 hours
Vertical rise: 1,300 feet
Map: NY–NJTC Catskill Trails Map #41

To reach this quiet and isolated pair of overlooks, now marked only as a snowmobile and horse trail, you travel the historic Old Mountain Road through Rip Van Winkle Hollow, which, notes Van Zandt, "was to become the classic approach to the great scenic domain of the Catskill Mountain House for almost all the remaining years of the nineteenth century." The road had its beginning in 1823 as a tannery road and stage coach route to Charles L. Beach's Catskill Mountain House. It remained a stage route until the railroad came in the 1880s which resulted in its eventual abandonment.

By 1931, H. A. Haring wrote in *Our Catskill Mountains* that the road "is impassable for any sort of vehicle, but is endlessly charming for the hiker who is equal to an ascent of 2,000 feet within a walking distance of five miles." The road has been repaired since, and new bridges are in place for the modern hiker.

Begin at the western end of the Mountain Turnpike Road, which you will find by turning right in Palenville on Bogart Road, the first right after the light on NY 23A as you are driving west. Follow Bogart Road for 2.5 miles to a four-way intersection with Mountain Turnpike Road

at Pelham's four corners (the portion to the right is dirt). There are some old trail signs here that, at this writing, are decayed badly. Turn left, and go one mile to the end of Mountain Turnpike Road, where you can park. You will see the snowmobile trail markers as the road turns to dirt and curves uphill into Rip Van Winkle Hollow.

As you begin, you follow Stony Brook on the left, which for the first mile of trail skirts a deep hemlock ravine. Continuing uphill over a roadway that is still manageable for four-wheel drive vehicles, you cross Black Snake Bridge within one-half mile. A hardwood forest slopes up to your right toward the escarpment, while the ravine, pitching steeply down to your left, slowly rises to intersect the trail at the horseshoe turn in Sleepy Hollow, where you see the old stone foundations of The Rip Van Winkle House. The one-mile distance to this point will take you a half hour of uphill hiking, so you may enjoy a stop here, the traditional resting place for coach travelers to the Mountain House.

Every effort was made to assure guests that this was the spot where Rip encountered the strange crew of Henry Hudson's Half Moon. Nearby was the rock upon which he took his famous slumber, and a tree could be pointed out beneath which the bones of his dog Wolf were "discovered." Haring recorded that "every summer visitors in hundreds scrambled up the perpendicular continuation of Sleepy Hollow in search of the 'flats' where Hendrick Hudson's gnomes thunderously rolled the balls in their game of ninepins." In fact, Washington Irving is not specific as to the location of the events in the legend, which appealed to the romantic mind for its very vagueness and mystery. He never visited the Catskills until 1832, twelve years after the publication of the story.

Continue from here on the half-mile-long Dead Ox Hill, going steadily uphill through hardwoods toward the little Pine Orchard and Cape Horn. You reach Cape Horn within thirty minutes of Sleepy Hollow, to find a stone fireplace and rough campsite. From Cape Horn, views to the east are fair, with the Taconics and the river valley visible. Make a 180-degree right turn here, onto the Short Level, which takes you up a moderate

grade to another horseshoe bend in 0.3 mile, or ten minutes.

Now you turn toward the north, then switch back south to Featherbed Hill. This path also is shown on an 1876 map drawn by Walton Van Loan, entitled "Map of All Points of Interest Within Four Miles of the Catskill Mountain House." You can get a photocopy of it at the Haines Falls Library. Van Loan's representation of this particular area, specifically from the Saxe Farm at the end of Mountain Turnpike Road to Palenville Overlook, while not entirely reliable, accurately shows this section of the trail.

Many of the trails, however, are rerouted or abandoned. Other maps showing this trail are the Walking News's Hikers' Region Map Number 35 and the New York State DEC's "Horse Trails in New York State."

The trail throughout is so well marked that you will have no trouble following it. From Featherbed Hill, you walk the next 1.5 miles uphill through a hardwood forest until reaching a Y in the trail. Take a

left at this Y. This point is known as the Long Level, where the grade becomes flatter as it approaches the bend in the road. If you wish to see the bend, continue straight 0.3 mile, but it is no longer a scenic attraction since the destruction of the Mountain House. There is a limited view of Pine Orchard here. This was the most popular location for painting and etching the Mountain House as it was seen in detail by visitors on the stage route. The classic scenic points favored by nineteenth-century artists were from the north, and above the hotel, in the neighborhood of Sunset Rock and North Point (see North Point Loop hike). Most of the prints can be seen at Haines Falls Library. You'll observe that the romantic painter intensified and exaggerated scenes to produce effect. Thomas Cole believed "the subject [of art] should be pure and lofty, . . . an impressive lesson must be taught, an important scene illustrated — a moral, religious or poetic effect be produced on the mind."

At the Y you follow a steep downhill grade left to the northeast, which switches back almost immediately to the south. In a few minutes you cross the open gash that runs up the mountain — the abandoned Otis Elevated Railroad track. Opened in 1892, this incline railway saved from three to four hours' stage time for the trip to the Catskill Mountain House, during the crucial period when the supremacy of Charles L. Beach's domain was being challenged by other resorts. Lack of patronage and the advent of automobile travel caused the railway to be closed in 1918, when its rails and cables were sold to the government for weapons manufacturing. The bare scrape it left in the escarpment can be seen for miles.

After crossing the railway clearing, the trail narrows through a forest of mixed hardwoods and continues along, flat and featureless (except for limited views through the trees to the east) until you reach a fork within twenty minutes. Take the right fork. One hundred feet beyond is a posted trail junction with a sign to Halfway House Lookout (0.45 mile), which is also Palenville Overlook. Follow this trail about ten or fifteen minutes on level terrain, and suddenly you'll stand over the abyssal depth of Kaaterskill Clove, with the village of Palenville below and remarkable views of Kaaterskill High Peak and Roundtop. To the west is Indian Head or Point of Rocks, which can be reached by bushwhacking along the cliff edge. A rough, unmarked trail exists at this time, but it is not continuous. By keeping the canyon to your left, it is difficult to get lost, though, and the extra diversion is worth the ten-minute walk.

These grassy, open areas are ideal spots for picnicking, sketching, photographing, camping, or simply pondering. The vertical drops are extremely dangerous here, so be cautious.

Indian Head (not to be confused with the Devil's Path mountain of that name) is a profile rock, and from More's Bridge in Kaaterskill Clove (just below Fawn's Leap) it does resemble a head. As you face the south from Indian Head, the bridge is visible on your right, far below. It is the second bridge west of Palenville.

When you have enjoyed this place to your satisfaction, you can return the way you came. Before leaving, if you should wish to rest in the bewitching silence, high above the birthplace of Rip Van Winkle, be careful lest you too should sleep away a lifetime.

Kaaterskill High Peak

Distance: 9 miles
Time: 6 hours
Vertical rise: 2,455 feet
Map: NY–NJTC Catskill Trails Map #41

High Peak was far more popular one hundred years ago during the hotel heydays than it is today. Then the Catskill boundaries were exaggerated by hotel magnates who did everything possible to convince visitors that their establishment was indeed positioned in the heart of the Catskills. High Peak was considered the highest mountain in the range until Arnold Guyot reduced it to a lowly twenty-third on the list of Catskill peaks (actually it is twenty-first). Guyot's map and report on the Catskills, published in 1879 and 1880, was produced when he was writing textbooks and building a foundation for the United States Weather Bureau. His formidable authority and statements then were considered absolute; at the same time he challenged local belief to the point that many people claimed his findings were in scientific error.

Guyot had believed Black Top (3980 feet) to be the highest in the range, but in 1871 he assigned that rank to Hunter Mountain (4040 feet). By 1872 he had determined that Slide (4180 feet) in fact was king of the Catskills, a finding that qualified the Shandaken Mountains as geological members of the Catskills.

From the Hudson Valley, High Peak does appear to be the highest mountain on the skyline. Its elliptic shape betrays it from north, east, and south, and it can be identified further by its lower westerly neighbor, Round Top (3440 feet), which stands like a dorsal fin in High Peak's shadow. Longstreth, in his volume *The Catskills*, describes High Peak and Round Top from the Hotel Kaaterskill as "sublime breakers just ready to topple over in a universal thunder of white foam." James Fenimore Cooper, in his legendary Leatherstocking novel, *The Pioneers,* quotes the hero as stating: "Well, there's High-peak and the Round-top which lay back like a father and mother among their children, seeing they are far above all the other hills."

While it is evident from guidebooks and maps of the golden era that Kaaterskill was a popular climbing destination, the mountain has since enjoyed such inconspicuousness that not even a state-marked trail crosses its summit. At this time, a snowmobile trail circles both High Peak and Round Top, providing access to High Peak's summit trail. Round Top is trailless. Because there is only a vague (but negotiable) trail to High Peak from this well-defined snowmobile trail, it should be regarded as a strenuous and

Twin, right, and Indian Head from Kaaterskill High Peak

© 1983 New York–New Jersey Trail Conference

a dirt road appears on the left with red and yellow snowmobile trail markers. *(Here you will also see the blue and white Long Path discs that mark a new trail to Palenville.)* The best parking is ahead, across a stone bridge with iron guard rails that skirts a deep, dangerous clove. A large gravel parking lot on the right will accommodate several cars.

Follow the snowmobile trail uphill through a dense hardwood forest, mixed with rich stands of hemlock, passing old stone walls on your left, and listening (in season) to a tumbling creek on your right. In about twenty-five minutes you will reach a fork where arrows indicate you turn right, following the snowmobile trail, which is washed out in places but consistently marked. In less than ten minutes you will reach another fork. Go right, through a forest of large oaks and other hardwood, where hemlock, viburnum, yellow violets, and trout lilies form a colorful understory. The trail is relatively level for the next twenty minutes until you reach a short timber bridge crossing into a swampy area between two shallow creeks. Another timber bridge is ahead within minutes, which you will cross after passing through this pretty spruce and fir swamp on a sodden trail of old corduroy and the spongy root systems of balsam fir.

Leaving the swamp, the trail heads uphill into a hardwood area where you may have to step over blowdowns—normally cleared on a regular basis, but rarely in early spring, the best time to climb High Peak. You will begin to see beech trees, blue violets, and some remarkably large hemlock and maple. Wildlife is abundant. Porcupines will scuttle away as you approach; owls will scrutinize you with haunting whispers as you rest. Here, amid the spring beauties, you can look south at Plattekill Mountain, and northwest at the shoulder of High Peak. Within forty minutes of leaving the swamp, in-

challenging hike that requires direction-finding skills, a map, and a compass. It also is a very quiet piece of country, even when the neighboring trails to the south and north (the Devil's Path and Escarpment Trails, respectively) traditionally are crowded. Camping opportunities are exceptional, water is normally abundant, and the views, although not frequent, are one of High Peak's best-kept secrets.

The trail begins at the top of Platte Clove, which can be reached most easily from Tannersville. Going west out of Tannersville, find the Bloomer Road (County Route 16) on your left at 1.5 miles. Follow this road heading back east for six miles, passing state trail signs into the Devil's Path Range on your right. Just past the New York City Police Camp site, cluding time for a good break, the trail will level out into a birch forest with scattered evergreens. This can be a wet area, of alpine quality with stands of solid conifer, cleared blowdown, and old corduroy. (The white markers with yellow centers that you see along the way eventually will disappear.)

After forty-five minutes of traversing this flat, swampy section of trail, which in spring is uncomfortably wet in places, turn sharply left, still following the snowmobile markers. *(If you are hiking the Long Path, the new trail to Palenville via Buttermilk Falls and Wildcat Ravine forks to the right off the described route at this point. This trail is significant because it completes the Long Path in the Catskills.)* The trail leads uphill here, and within five minutes you reach a trail junction with several signs describing the loop around Kaaterskill and Round Top and the direction back to Platte Clove Road. Turn right (west). There is no sign indicating a trail to High Peak's summit, so at this time you must be very alert to pick it up on your left. Within 500 feet or more, blue blazes can be seen off the trail in a southerly direction. You may have to search momentarily to see these; the blazes are old Long Path—colored (aqua-blue) paint, but the trail is not officially maintained as the Long Path at this writing.

In the spring, when water is running down the mountain, and when seasonal streambeds are still visible, you'll find a capillary creek at this junction. Shortly after this creek, you'll cross another one, and just before crossing a third you'll see the blazes on your left. Now look into the forest for a couple of hundred feet if you don't see a blaze right away. Once you've found the marks, follow uphill, looking for blazes on rocks and trees, into an area of steep ledges and rock-strewn, moss-cloaked forest.

An hour or more of strenuous hiking will take you across several ledges and through many tangled blowdowns as you reach the summit. You will get some views to the north of Kaaterskill Clove and the surrounding mountains, but mainly these are obscured by trees.

You will know you've achieved High Peak's summit when you reach a flat area among the evergreens, where benchmarks can be studied in the stone. To reach Hurricane Ledge and its remarkable views, follow the trail for another fifteen minutes, which will bring you to a large expanse of grassy, open terrain with an east-to-west, south-facing aspect. The view is rare, including a variety of topography from the Hudson River Valley, the Shawangunks, the Hudson Highlands, and the immediate Catskills. The ledge is a fine place to snooze, snack, photograph, or bivouac.

High Peak and Round Top are often present in Hudson River School paintings of the nineteenth century as background or subject matter, particularly in scenes from the Catskill Mountain House area. One of the finest representations of Kaaterskill High Peak appears in Thomas Cole's "Sunny Morning on the Hudson," which depicts a highly romanticized version of High Peak from the vicinity of Round Top. While it can be argued that the peak is not Kaaterskill, climb Round Top with a photocopy of the painting, and you will have little doubt that it is.

Plateau from Stony Clove

Distance: 6 miles
Time: 6 hours
Vertical rise: 1,840 feet
Map: NY–NJTC Catskill Trails Map #41

"If you will believe me that the Stony Clove is a pastoral of lyric beauty with one dramatic climax, instead of the roaring bloody gulch of the fictional folders, hope that you will also believe that its beauties cannot be more than skimmed by him who trusts only to steam or gasoline for his scenic memories."

So wrote T. Morris Longstreth in his 1918 classic, *The Catskills,* which he promised to be free of exaggeration. No hiker who ascends the steep paths of Stony Clove would disagree.

It is curious also to read Longstreth's impressions of quaint Phoenicia, which you should visit when you descend Plateau summit. He describes it as the "nerve center" of the Catskills, lying at the "cross-roads of Nature." He likes the "clean" and "painted" shops and applauds the lack of the commercial development that is so typical of some small Catskill villages today, a blight that Longstreth recognized even in 1918. What he says is still true, for Phoenicia, which lies within the clove's southerly access, remains a tidy, scenic, and unpretentious retreat.

Stony Clove notch is a narrow mountain pass with all the rugged visual appeal that Longstreth promises. It is

formed by the long ridge of Plateau meeting with that of Hunter and holds at its apex the teardrop of Notch Lake and the Devil's Tombstone State Campground, where the Devil's Path Trail crosses NY 214. To locate the trailhead, drive south on NY 214 from NY 23A between Hunter and Tannersville, and go three miles to the south end of Notch Lake. Or from the south at Phoenicia and NY 28, go north on NY 214 nine miles. Park at Notch Lake and cross the road to the east, climbing the log staircase where you will find the trail sign. Plateau summit is indicated at one mile, but a look at your map will tell you that the actual summit is on the east end of Plateau's red-marked long ridge at 3840 feet, a good 2.5 miles from the trailhead. (By now you know you should be skeptical about state trail signs.) What you will discover at the mile mark, although not the summit, will please you more than the actual summit, which is boreal and enclosed.

The spot that some well-meaning DEC employee considered as Plateau's summit is an outstanding viewpoint at 3600 feet—one that often is ranked in the hierarchy of Catskill vistas. Don't be misled if the black star indicating a viewpoint does not appear on your NY–NJTC map. The view is there, along with several others farther east.

Begin the climb by going uphill over rocky terrain into a tall forest of young hardwood. A few minutes ahead, take some time to observe a slide to your left with a few large slabs and broken talus heaped up beneath it. A short (200-foot) spur trail leads you to it. Continuing on the red trail, you'll pass another short, unmarked spur to the right, which leads to a good campsite near a stream. After this point the main trail gets very steep, with makeshift stone steps to aid your ascent. In ten minutes or more, as you climb over roots and rocks, you'll encounter more slides to your left (which are now stable and safe) and views to your right. Continue amid birch and cherry trees for ten minutes until you reach an area that has been cleared to provide a view. Several trees have been topped, providing views of Wittenberg, Cornell, Friday, Peekamoose and Table, Panther, and beyond.

These good views vanish as the trail turns north, with spring beauties and red trillium sprinkled sparingly along its edge. If the trillium is in bloom during your visit, you might be surprised at its putrid scent, one that is unbecoming to such a pretty flower. Blooming as it does in very early spring, the trillium's stench attracts pollinating insects in search of decomposing flesh. For this reason it is called a "carrion" flower. All species of trillium are rare, protected, and *may not* be picked. In the spring you also will see in bloom the very pretty viburnum, or hobblebush, with its large, heart-shaped leaves, a favorite deer food.

On this flat section of trail, you can look back west for occasional views of Hunter Mountain. You will cross the 3500-foot mark and perhaps see a sign indicating this point. In another ten minutes you will traverse some ledges, which take you gradually up and onto the very scenic overlook on Plateau's western end. This is a 180-degree view, reaching across the range from Colonel's Chair to Hunter, West Hunter, West Kill, the High Peaks, and into the Ashokan Reservoir.

There are several illegal campsites in this area, which you pass as you follow the trail around through the east. The New York State Department of Environmental Conservation requires that hikers

140 *Eastern Catskills*

"camp and build open fires only below 3500 feet." An unobstructed overlook on the ridge's north shoulder surveys the Blackheads, North Point, South Mountain, Round Top, Kaaterskill High Peak, and down into Platte Clove. Hard to your right you will see Spruce Top and then Sugar Loaf with its long ridgeline plunging into Mink Hollow to meet the Roaring Kill and Schoharie. At this lookout there is a large apparently balancing rock upon which a crude rising sun is carved. Beneath it we found a fulcrum stone and a broken timber, suggesting that boulder-levering is not a forgotten pastime. Most of the good balanced rocks were pushed into their present locations a century ago by visitors to the mountain houses.

Continue on the flat ridge over a good trail for another five minutes until you reach an overlook with the same northerly views. Trees here also have been cut to provide an uninterrupted view. Many blown-down conifers lie upon the ridge, much like bleached whale bone against the contrast of verdant life.

Within five or ten minutes you will reach an attractive but over-used campsite with "no camping" postings. Continue through a forest of large spruce and fir, where the trail switches to the ridge's south side. You begin to go uphill slightly in a few minutes, and within another ten minutes witness a thick understory of balsam beneath a dead overstory. The trail here is reminiscent of Indian Head but not so enclosed. Whipped winds tear along the thin ridge as you peer through trees into Silver Hollow and Stony Clove. The forest remains coniferous on this long walk to the summit; it lends a somehow nostalgic feel, maybe reminding you of favorite walks in places far away: the Pacific Crest, the Whites, the Maine coast. They all come to mind.

In twenty minutes you will reach the summit, which you'll recognize only by a ninety-degree left turn where the trail turns south to east. Follow it for another fifteen minutes to your final destination—a rock looking east. Jump across a shallow crevasse and survey Sugar Loaf, Kaaterskill High Point, Round Top, North Point, North Mountain, Overlook, and part of Twin. The view is limited compared to the one you had farther west, but it gives the hiker an intimate feeling for the heart of the Devil's Path. It is a sight unavailable to "him who trusts only to steam or gasoline for his scenic memories."

Return the way you came, and keep an ear open for the "grrrooook, grrroook, grrroook" of nesting ravens.

Indian Head Loop

Distance: 6 miles
Time: 4½ hours
Vertical rise: 1,573 feet
Map: NY–NJTC Catskill Trails Map #41

Indian Head is a beguiling triad of peaks, which make up a profile mountain that can be seen from afar as a face looking skyward. The profile is more impressionistic than real, more caricature than exact, very much in the cigarstore Indian style. It is best seen from the north or east, from the Taconics or from Olana, Frederic Church's Persian castle in Hudson, and from the New York State Thruway and the surrounding valleys. Thomas Cole painted it in 1843 in "River in the Catskills," the mountain set in vague repose beyond the dark ridges running southeast from Kaaterskill High Peak.

Indian Head is a contender for the position of most rugged and intriguing of the Devil's Path mountains. Its summit ridge is so boreal, so completely enclosed by thick spruce and fir, that you are never certain you are on a mountain at all, but feel lost in a sea of endless, aromatic brush. The mountain yields its claustraphobic clutches piecemeal, giving you some extra rugged views every now and then to lure you onward.

To reach the trailhead, turn south off NY 23A at the (only) light in Tannersville on County Route 16. At 1.3 miles this road intersects the Bloomer Road, on which you turn left. Within 0.4 mile you

will reach a Y where you bear left on Platte Clove Mountain Road. At three miles you pass Dale Lane on the right (trail to Sugarloaf, Twin, Pecoy Notch). Stay on Platte Clove Mountain Road, and in one mile you'll see Prediger Road on the right. Follow it 0.25 mile to the trail.

Here you will see signs on the red trail to Indian Head Mountain, Dolan Notch, and Echo Lake. The mileages shown from the trail junction (Indian Head 3.35, Dolan Notch 3.80) are correct for taking the trail from east to west, not from west to east as you will do.

The foot trail leads you into the forest over a timber bridge across one of several lively creeks that will keep you company until higher elevations are reached. Follow the self-guiding and well-marked old road uphill, reaching the trail register within 500 feet. Maps are (at this time) posted here. Within ten minutes you pass a stream on your right, and a trail junction appears. Bear right on the blue trail, which shows Dolan's Notch at 2.2 and Indian Head at 2.65 miles. Don't be mislead by the lean-to arrow on the red trail; there is no closer shelter than a lean-to 1.5 miles away at Devil's Kitchen. (As a general rule of thumb, never place absolute trust in state trail signs.)

On the blue trail to Dolan's Notch, which is a section of the Long Path, you'll go uphill slightly over a rocky trail with exposed tree roots, an occasional large hemlock, and a few huge cherry trees. To your right, in a northerly direction, you can see Kaaterskill High Peak and Roundtop Mountain through the trees in the spring. The trail is not strenuous yet, as you slowly bend to the south, getting a view of Twin's northerly shoulder up to your right.

The trail becomes eroded badly in places where run-off has created a temporary stream bed. The various streams you encounter, and the one you can hear in the ravine just west of you, form the easternmost headwaters of the Schoharie Creek.

As you continue along a steeper section of the trail, you'll have a peak at Indian Head on your left (southeast) and will see more of Twin to the right. Climbing higher, about forty-five minutes into your hike (1.5 miles), you can look back (north) at Kaaterskill High Peak, Roundtop, and the Blackhead Range. Within ten or fifteen minutes more you will be happy to arrive at the notch for some rest before the steep summit climb.

Here the Long Path intersects with the Devil's Path, showing Indian Head at (a rugged) 0.45 mile, and Platte Clove Mountain Road (your exit route) at 3.95 miles. Take some time to explore here, and don't miss a walk into the notch, which you can see from the trail junction. Walk into the V as far as you can safely go for a good look at the Esopus Valley and some of the southern Catskills. For less restricted views to the south, follow the rim of the notch to the west, via a fairly well-trodden herd path, to a steep and dangerous cliff that forms the west side of the V on the notch. More views are possible if you pursue the meandering path, which eventually dead-ends. Jimmy Dolan's Notch is a local favorite. It is in every sense a classic notch, a symmetrical cut through the mountain that is scattered with large boulders and crumbling rock shelves, an ancient river canyon from which the waters have long since run off.

The trail climbs and eases alternately as you struggle uphill from the notch, going east. After a half hour of this terrace climbing, the trail, thick with hemlock and balsam, will flatten suddenly. This is the only indication that you have

Looking south through Jimmy Dolan Notch

reached the summit, completely surrounded by trees and with no view.
Within five minutes you go downhill
slightly, to another flat area where huge,
climax spruce trees soar above. A few
enticing ledges here and there on your
right provide limited views south.

Continue along through a pure evergreen forest. Some restricted views of the
Sawkill Valley are available to the south if
you want to push your way through the
trees and explore a little.

You are now descending to the middle
knoll, from the forehead (summit) to the
eyebrow of the Indian Head. On the eastern end of the middle knoll, you reach a
high overlook that juts out to the east
with a vertical, dangerous drop, at 3,200

feet above sea level. A near 180-degree view reveals the Ashokan, Shawangunks, Overlook, the Hudson (part of which is obstructed by the east knoll, or nose) and the Highlands, Taconics, and Berkshires. You are roughly midway through the hike, with three miles behind you.

From here follow cautiously down a very steep section of trail into a shallow saddle separating the eyebrow and nose. Within ten minutes you encounter another thick stand of fir that would be difficult, if not impossible, to walk through without a trail. Going uphill, and leveling out onto the nose, in ten minutes or so you will reach a spot where a view has been cut. The result is an outstanding look at the Catskills High Peaks area, running from Ashokan High Point over to Slide and beyond. In this outstanding collection of peaks are also Peekamoose and Table, Lone, Rocky, Balsam Cap, Samuels, Friday, Wittenberg, Cornell, Giant Ledge, Panther, and many more.

Within a few minutes of leaving this area, you will swing toward the north, skirting the nose's easterly rim, which will give you a look at Plattekill's western shoulder. With fair views to the east along the trail, you'll have the opportunity to look deep into Platte Clove, and within five minutes you'll reach Outlook Rock, which has also been cut over to provide views to the north and a previously unavailable look at the Blackhead Mountains. This is the last scenic overlook before the plunge into the valley.

After twenty minutes or so of hiking downhill, with diminishing views to the east, you may find the trail wet as it terraces down, level for a way, then steep again. The footing is red shale and some broken conglomerate. The majestic stands of large virgin hemlock here, some over thirty inches in diameter, reflect the magnificence that was primordial forest.

The tanbark era in the Catskills, which ran from about 1830 to 1870, resulted in the near deforestation of such hemlock. Hemlock bark, rich in tannin, was used in leather tanning. Trees could be peeled profitably only to the first branch, so much of the tree bark was wasted, and perhaps less than one percent of the lumber was used. Most of the trees were left to rot. In H. A. Haring's estimation, "from three to ten hemlocks were felled to obtain a cord of bark (128 cu. ft.). . . . Probably, in the life of the industry, one hemlock was cut down for each hide tanned into leather. . . . Col. Pratt, at Prattsville, turned out more than two million hides" during the lifespan of his tannery. With at least sixty tanneries running for forty years, you get an idea of the vast number of trees involved. The trees here are some of the largest hemlocks you will ever see in the Catskills. Chances are they were in their vigorous youth as the industry waned.

Within a half hour to forty minutes of leaving the nose, you reach a trail junction. To your right at 0.2 mile is Devil's Kitchen lean-to, and Echo Lake (2.8). To your left, two routes lead to Platte Clove Mountain Road. About 500 feet down this trail, after you've turned left, the red trail dodges back into the woods, going left. Watch closely for this, for it's not too obvious. Don't go straight on the CCCD (Catskill Center for Conservation and Development) trail, or you'll wind up east of Prediger Road.

Turning left, or northeast, and back into deep hemlock woods, the trail takes you uphill slightly. In ten or fifteen minutes you reach a creek with a set of log stairs in place, which you cross, continuing through a fern glade, crossing another small stream and reaching the trail junction where you took the blue trail. The one-mile section of trail from Devil's Kitchen will take you about twenty-five minutes. Turn right, and you are back at the parking lot in a few minutes.

Twin Mountain

Distance: 4 miles
Time: 5–6 hours
Vertical rise: 1,900 feet
Map: NY–NJTC Catskill Trails Map #41

Twin is one of the Devil's Path mountains, those craggy and tempestuous summits that you see crowding the western sky as you drive between Catskill and Saugerties on the New York Thruway.

Forming the southeastern shoulder of the northern Catskills is Overlook and its Minister's Face, which juts into the valley, looking from a distance like a coastal headland. the ridge running north from Overlook is Plattekill Mountain (3,100 feet), which is fairly flat for several miles and of the same elevation as Overlook. This continuity is broken as the ridge turns 90 degrees to the west, and over the irregular horizon of Indian Head, Twin, Sugarloaf, and Plateau Mountains.

This is the Devil's Path. Falling away to the north are the deep, stone-ravaged depths of the Devil's Kitchen. To the south is the town of Woodstock; to the west the Path drops suddenly into Stony Clove Notch. Perhaps because they are comparatively easy for the hiker, or because they lack the deep cavernous cloves so feared by the early Dutch settlers, Overlook and Plattekill are not included in colloquial descriptions of the Devil's Path mountains. Instead, the diabolical distinction is given to the mountains that run from Indian Head to

Hunter. In recent years, West Kill has been included in the trail system to challenge hikers on what has become the most rugged and longest continuous trail network in the Catskills, with a total distance of twenty-four miles. This can be lengthened by an additional 5.5 miles to include Plattekill and Overlook, finishing (or beginning) in Meads.

While the Devil's Path in its entirety, from Platte Clove to Spruceton, is a popular and strenuous weekend outing for serious backpackers, any single mountain in the chain can be hiked in a day or less. At the same time, the Devil's Path is aptly named for its tormenting ascents, its profusion of rock, its abrupt visual contrasts, its dark hemlock corridors and false peaks. You will be rewarded on the trail with unusual feelings of isolation and with splendid views.

Many short side trails join the main ridge trail of the Devil's Path, predominantly from the north. They provide not only short hikes into an otherwise remote series of higher elevation peaks but also easy bail-out routes in the event of emergency or foul weather.

Twin is best hiked from the Pecoy Notch Trail, which ascends gradually from the Schoharie Creek along Platte

Clove Mountain Road. From Bloomer Road, 1.75 miles west of Tannersville on NY 23A, travel southeast on Platte Clove Mountain Road to the trail sign on Dale Lane Road (4.5 miles). Turn right here, and continue straight onto Wase Road, which leads in one mile to the trailhead. Tannersville can be reached from the south via the NYS Thruway and routes to Hunter (NY 32A and NY 23A) or from Phoenicia and Woodstock, which are both west of Kingston off NY 28A, by following scenic NY 214 through Stony Clove and turning right on NY 23A, twelve miles north of Phoenicia.

From the trailhead it is 1.2 miles to Pecoy Notch, where the trail branches west to Sugarloaf and east to Twin, another half-mile farther. This presents the possibility of hiking Sugarloaf as well as Twin in a one-day outing. Keep in mind the additional two miles and a cumulative elevation gain of 2,500 feet. Twin has the superior view, however, and you can save Sugarloaf for a later hike that could include a section of the Mink Hollow Trail and a look at the boreal Plateau Mountain.

Following trail markers in two shades of blue—both light and dark are used interchangeably at this time—walk to the trail register and sign in. Registering is not only a safety precaution but also a vital tool for determining public use of the Forest Preserve.

The beginning of this trail can be wet in early spring, as it follows an eroded gully through a poorly drained hemlock and mixed hardwood forest. Tiptoe across a small bog, which is alive with peepers in April, and continue on higher ground into stands of northern hardwood and an occasional striped maple. Club moss and trillium line the trail. At around the 2,400-foot elevation, less than a mile into the hike, you will see a beaver pond 300 feet or so to the west (right). The pond, which may be dry in summer,

© 1983 New York–New Jersey Trail Conference

abuts the relatively featureless footpath and makes an interesting diversion. It can be circled in fifteen or twenty minutes, allowing you to rejoin the trail again by turning east at the pond's southern edge. Beaver activity is diminishing in this pond that feeds the Schoharie, but several dams and lodges might be seen still, and the several-acre expanse of rotting timber will be evident for years. The pond has a quiet, primordial spirit about it, making a welcome stopover. Its waters are contained by a sudden elevation gain at its most southern point, where its feeding creek trickles down from Sugarloaf. As you regain the trail and hike uphill you will begin to get views to the north of Thomas Cole, Black Dome, and Blackhead, left to right, collectively known as the Blackhead Range.

At 1.2 miles, after about an hour's leisurely hiking, you reach Pecoy Notch, and the ridge trail of the Devil's Path. To the left on this section of the Long Path is Twin at one-half mile with an additional 987-foot vertical rise.

There is no trail out of Pecoy Notch to the south, only a profusion of tumble-down boulders and twisted logs. This is one of the notches, along with its easterly neighbor Jimmy Dolan Notch, that can be seen as bright bare scrapes from points as far south as the Shawangunks.

Turn left and go uphill over a good trail through scrubby beech, birch, and maple. The incline is steep with a west-erly aspect, soon exposing Sugarloaf and beyond it Hunter and its fire tower. You pass a large rock overhang that has been heavily used by hikers and is a convenient shelter in the event of rain. Al-though steep in places, the trail is easy and interesting to walk, even if you'll find yourself breathing heavily and resting fre-quently. Suddenly, through a balsam-thick shoulder of the mountain you will see views opening up to the south, the vertical ledges of stone on your path fi-nally subsiding to a series of flat outcrop-pings that form the north summit of Twin.

From this point the view is very good, extending as far south and southwest as the eye can see, but it is blocked to the north and east by mountains in the 3,500-foot class. From this southerly ex-posure you can survey the southern Cat-skills' high peaks just west of the Asho-kan Reservoir. You should recognize

Ashokan High Point, Samuels Point, Fri-day, Wittenberg, Cornell, Panther, Giant Ledge, Balsam Cap, Balsam Lake Moun-tain, and Graham, with many lower sur-rounding peaks identifiable with the aid of map and compass. You will also have a close look at the foreground mountains, Tremper, Carl, and Olderbark (west to east). During run-off, listen closely and you might hear the noisy waters of the Sawkill or Mink Hollow Brook. Cooper Lake, part of Kingston's water supply, is visible five miles south-southwest of you, with Mount Tobias on its right.

The southerly summit of Twin is an easy half-mile hike from here through a saddle of dense coniferous forest, which brings you to another flat rock overlook, facing south. Views to the east are of the Hudson River Valley and much of the river itself. From here nearly the entire Ashokan Reservoir is visible, as well as the Shawangunks. On a clear day, be-yond them, you can even see scattered hills of the Hudson Highlands.

You'll want to visit both of Twin's sum-mits to take in the variety of views that one cannot offer individually. If you have a lunch, plan to enjoy it at the more ex-pansive southerly summit. Return the way you came, and while descending the north summit, about halfway down, you can test your lungs against the echoes from Sugarloaf.

Huckleberry Point

Distance: 3.5 miles
Time: 2 hours
Vertical rise: 350 feet
Map: NY–NJTC Catskill Trails Map #41

Huckleberry Point is a delightful, little-known and out-of-the-way day hike in one of the Catskill's quietest corners. This small outcropping of rock hangs over the Hudson Valley, where the Plattekill Creek runs out of Platte Clove. It commands an intimate view of both, and it is seldom visited by hikers who are not familiar with the area's secret footpaths. The point is appreciated locally, though, and if you ask around on a sunny weekend you may be directed to several access alternatives that cross private lands. The only public trail access is via the snowmobile trail that runs around Kaaterskill High Peak, which you follow for a short distance. (See that hike for directions to the trailhead.) Huckleberry is the ideal picnicking point, suitable to those days when an easy hike with a quiet, scenic payoff is the goal.

Follow the snowmobile trail markers, which are both red and yellow, to an arrow pointing to the right, which you should reach within twenty-five minutes of leaving the paved road. After turning here, you will find another turn to the right (in less than ten minutes) indicating the continuation of the snowmobile trail.

Within four to five minutes, only a short distance from the junction, the trail will begin to turn north slightly. Looking very

carefully to your right at this point, locate the white markers with the red dot in the middle. These are markers put up by a group of hikers known as the Nature Friends. The markers are old rusting tin can bottoms that may vary in size, color, and condition. The trail is not used much, but the marking is reliable and easily followed by careful eyes. This will be quite a change if you are accustomed only to the worn, self-leading, state-marked trials, so stay alert and watch the markers closely.

When you have located the Nature Friends' trail, follow it east (right) through a level hardwood forest with a hemlock understory. You see many signs of early settlement: stone piles, walls, and perhaps an old foundation or two. The trail is remarkably clean—free of litter and blowdowns. Within several minutes you go slightly downhill, the trail becomes easier to follow, and you reach a tiny, clear brook that can be several feet deep during run-off. Find a safe place to ford, and continue directly on the other side toward the point. Don't make the mistake of following one of the old overgrown skid roads you may see at this point. Be sure you follow the white and red markers.

A few minutes from the stream you

downhill, yielding early spring views of the Devil's Path peaks, including Overlook (see if you can spot the fire tower), Indian Head, Twin, Sugarloaf, and Plattekill.

Within a half-hour of starting the Nature Friends' trail at the snowmobile trail, you enter a forest primarily of pitch pine with some red and white pine. Large rocks and a needle-covered forest floor color the scene, which may interest you in camping out. There are several natural campsites here, but be careful with fire in the soft subsoil beneath the pines.

Markers continue through the forest, within moments leading to a southerly bend in the trail, where you begin to sense the abyss ahead. Suddenly, you reach the open rocks of the point, with the ridge running from Hunter visible before you. Overlook's Minister's Face, the eastern tip of the Ashokan, Mohonk, the Hudson Highlands, Kingston, Saugerties, the Taconics, and lands beyond are recognizable.

This is a great place to get close to large raptors—including ravens, hawks, and vultures who ride the updrafts against the cliff, rarely flapping their wings, oblivious to the rocks that are so rarely visited by people.

To avoid trespassing, return the way you came.

begin to climb slightly, crossing a narrow bridge into an oak and beech forest with laurel ground cover becoming very thick—possibly the thickest you'll see it in the Catskills. Don't be surprised if the trail markers suddenly lack the red center dot. You're still on the right trail. Don't worry about the ocean of laurel you must wade through, either, although it at times gives no indication of having a trail beneath it. The trail undulates easily up and

Kaaterskill Falls and the Cliff Walk

Distance: 5 miles
Time: 4 hours
Vertical rise: 300 feet
Map: NY–NJTC Catskill Trails Map #40

The trails in the North Lake area are the most popular, accessible, and historically significant in the Catskill range. At one time they were the most popular in North America. They encompass falls, cliff walks, and mountaintop vistas, and both North and South Lakes, their beaches, and public campgrounds. They constitute much of the twenty-four mile Escarpment Trail, traverse several old hotel sites, and make a variety of day or weekend outings very convenient and satisfying for both dawdlers and aggressive hikers. The views from the North Lake area's trails and popular observation points are famous in and of themselves, embellished in the prose of the romantic era to such an extent that any description of them risks redundancy.

The first and easily the most renowned of these passages can be found in James Fenimore Cooper's *The Pioneers*, in which Leatherstocking (Natty Bumppo) describes the view from Pine Orchard as one containing "all creation." The tale was written in 1823 the year the Catskill Mountain House was constructed. Leatherstocking says, "I saw the hills in the Hampshire grants, the highlands of the river, and all that God had done or man could do, far as the eye could

reach—you know that the Indians named me for my sight, lad [Leatherstocking refers to his nickname 'Hawkeye'], and from the flat on the top of that mountain I have often found the place where Albany stands."

Today, the North Lake trail network is a maze of both new and forgotten paths, roads, and horse trails, which were developed to support lucrative endeavors in tanning, quarrying, hotel building, logging, and railroading, following the earlier paths of hunters, trappers, fishermen, and surveyors.

Probably the most popular spot in the area, if not Pine Orchard itself, is Kaaterskill Falls. It is without peer if measured by the volume of literary and artistic attention given to it, and even Leatherstocking describes the falls as "the best piece of work that I've met within the woods."

To fully appreciate the falls, you must see them from below, where many hikers relax in the gathering mists of Spruce Creek. Because of extreme overuse and hazardous trail conditions, the Kaaterskill Falls access was made a dead-end trail in 1988. If you want to see the falls, park at the public parking area on NY 23A, which is 3.5 miles west of the intersection of NY 23A and NY 32A in Palenville, and the same distance east of Tannersville. Here you will be looking into Kaaterskill Clove and at Twilight and Santa Cruz Parks, with a good view of the valley below. Walk downhill (east) to the hairpin turn (a quarter-mile), where you'll find the trail signs on the road's north side. Follow the yellow trail markers over a heavily eroded path studded with exposed tree roots and large boulders. Once above Bastion Falls you might prefer to follow the creekbed instead of the less interesting trail. They are close to each other, and both lead to the falls. A round trip to the falls should take less than an hour.

You walk through a stand of virgin hemlock trees before reaching the falls at its lower basin, which is scattered with huge stones and some of the fragmented sections of the higher precipices. At 260 feet, these are the highest falls in New York State, consisting of two runs with vertical drops of 175 feet for the top and 85 feet for the lower run.

It was long ago fashionable, and is still possible today (although foolhardy), to walk behind the falling water of the upper amphitheater. Today this act, without the cabled walkways and stairs of the last century, involves considerable risk, and is not recommended. Kaaterskill Falls, once as popular as Niagara, fell out of favor after the epoch of the great hotels. Now they are so popular that during the summer months you might see over a hundred people picnicking on the upper ledges, which has led to fluctuating levels of litter and rock defacement.

The cliff walk (escarpment trail) begins on Scutt Road, several miles beyond the Kaaterskill Falls parking area. Drive uphill (west) about two miles and take the first right, following signs to North Lake. At the end of this road (4 miles) you will reach the North/South campground. Turn right on Scutt Road, which is just to the right before the campground entrance. Follow this road one mile to its terminus and park in the designated area. Follow the yellow trail to your right. Here you will see signs to Layman Monument, Inspiration Point, North Lake Campground, and NY 23A. Shortly beyond is the trail register in a stand of white birch trees. The trail becomes flatter here, and it is an easy fiteen-minute walk to Layman Monument, which commemorates a fire fighter who died at this spot in 1900.

A long, open series of overlooks on steep rock outcroppings follow, providing exciting views of the entire Kaaterskill Clove, of the precariously perched homes of Santa Cruz and Twilight Parks, and of the mountains immediately to the south, Kaaterskill High Peak and Round-top. You can look west to Hunter Mountain, Colonel's Chair, and the East Jewett range. Fifteen hundred feet below you, Kaaterskill Creek flows toward the Hudson.

The view gets better as you continue toward Sunset Rock and Inspiration Point, passing a yellow-marked trail that returns to Scutt Road and the red trail. Sunset Rock is the first large outcropping you reach after the trail junction. If you've timed your visit to coincide with the ap-pearance of the pinkster blossoms, and it is well worth it to do so (midMay to mid-June), you'll also see swallowtails, bronze coppers and cabbage butterflies alighting on them and on the many colored hawk-weeds and assorted wild flowers along the way. As you head for Inspiration Point, you dodge in and out of an oak and laurel forest over easy terrain.

After enjoying Inspiration Point, continue through the forest for another fifteen minutes of easy walking to reach Shorey Point, which you'll recognize by its horse trail markers and the trail signs to Scutt Road Corral (1.5 miles). Stay on the blue trail toward Boulder Rock (1.2 miles) and North Lake Campground (2.2 miles). There is no view from Shorey Point, and the trail becomes relatively featureless until you reach the Kaaterskill Hotel site on South Mountain, which takes about fifteen minutes. The site is neither marked

Graffiti—or art? Kaaterskill Falls (circa 1825)

nor obvious—it is an empty grassy knoll adjacent to the trail junction as you turn right toward Boulder Rock. The hotel was built in 1881 and burned in 1924.

Continue on the blue trail to Boulder Rock, and at 0.5 mile you reach a trail junction where the red trail shortcuts off to the left toward the Mountain House site. Avoid this trail, and continue following the blue markers. In a few moments you reach Split Rock, a large rock leaning away from the trail with a deep fissure cleaving it, and just beyond it, Boulder Rock. Views of the Hudson Valley here are outstanding, giving an idea of what's to come over at Pine Orchard.

You continue to have fine, far-reaching views of the Shawangunks, Taconics, Berkshires, and the escarpment, as you hike along toward Pine Orchard. Avoid the several intersecting, older, unmarked trails that now are closed because of erosion and hazardous situations, and keep to the trail. Within ten minutes you reach the north end of the red shortcut trail where a sign shows North Lake Campground at 0.9 mile. After a fifteen-minute walk through cool, dark forests of mixed hardwood, pine, and hemlock, you suddenly reach the large open ledge where the Mountain House stood. Here you can look north toward North Point, North Mountain, and Sunset Rock. There is a bench here, with a plaque commemorating the hotel, but there are no ruins, as earlier topographic maps might indicate. After being declared a menace to public safety, the Catskill Mountain House was burned on January 25, 1963, at 6 a.m., no longer to command its ephemeral view over "all creation."

At this point you have hiked for about two hours. To return to your car, you can go back the way you came, or you can follow a faster, shorter route via the North/South Lake service road, which you'll intercept just west of the hotel site. It can also be reached by following the blue trail that continues going north, dropping downhill to the top of the abandoned Otis Elevated Railroad Track, which runs up the mountain from Palenville. The road then runs from North Lake public beach along the south shores of both lakes (go left), and continues going west. Follow it until you see a sign for the Nordic Ski Trail. If you cross the earthworks dam at the west end of South Lake, you've gone too far. Keep looking to your left, and about twenty minutes from the hotel site, within sight of the lake, you'll see the yellow markers. This ski trail will take you downhill slightly to the Scutt Road Corral parking lot in less than 0.5 mile.

34

North Point

Distance: 7 miles
Time: 4½ hours
Vertical rise: 700 feet
Map: NY–NJTC Catskill Trails Map #40

This historic, scenic day hike begins in the heart of the North-South Lake State Campground and includes some of the best scenery available from anywhere along the eastern escarpment, and maybe the entire range.

To reach North Lake Campground, turn north from NY 23A onto O'Hara Road (County Route 18) in Haines Falls, and go straight ahead, 2.5 miles, to the gatehouse.

You may begin outside the campground entrance in order to avoid the minimal day-use fee charged at the front gate, but that trail (Rock Shelter Trail, yellow) is longer and less interesting than the recommended Mary's Glen Trail (red), which begins just 0.75 mile beyond the gatehouse.

Limited hikers' day-use parking is located at the Mary's Glen trailhead, which you will see on the left just beyond the Mary's Glen trail sign. Park and walk back to the sign, which shows Mary's Glen at 0.4 mile. There is another location in the North Lake area that has the name of Mary's Glen, or Glen Mary, just above Kaaterskill Falls on Lake Creek (Kaaterskill Creek). In both instances the placename remembers Mary Scribner, wife of Ira Scribner, who operated a saw-

mill on the creek. The Glen Mary Cottage was most likely where Henry David Thoreau, with William Ellery Channing, spoke of spending an evening in the early 1840s.

The Glen is a cool, sometimes wet and rocky, but easy trail that skirts a swampy area full of beaver signs. Go left when you reach the bottom of Ashley's Falls at 0.4 mile, where a spur trail continues for a short distance ahead into the stone rubble below the falls.

Hike along the trail indicating North Point at 1.3 miles, and stop to enjoy the falls before continuing. The hike in from the trailhead should take only fifteen or twenty minutes. Continue on the trail toward North Point, beneath an overstory of white birch, hemlock, and maple for another ten minutes, which will bring you to a four-way trail junction. Locate the red markers for Mary's Glen Trail, which is the continuation of the trail you are on, and follow it toward North Point (one mile). Passing a long ledge that sports a small waterfall during wet periods, climb above it through more ledgy terrain and into a flat, swampy, coniferous area. The swamp has swallowed up a piece of the trail here, where a "herd" detour is being created. You may still get your feet wet

on the new, peripheral route in spring. If the foliage allows, you might at this point be able to look high to your left (northwest) and see the ledges of North Point.

Within a half hour of leaving the trail junction you will reach another, where the blue trail (Escarpment Trail) on which you will be returning leads back to Artists Rock and the campground. Turn left here, onto the only continuously steep section of the trail. After fifteen minutes of strenuous and aerobic effort, you will see a white birch stand that precedes the large flat rocks and long views from North Point summit. Investigate views from various parts of the ledge: Windham High Peak, Burnt Knob and Acra Point, Blackhead and Round Top to the north; the Hudson Valley toward Albany, to the east through the Taconics and Berkshires; and south across the highlands and into the escarpment, where North and South Lake lie like spilled quicksilver under the shadows of Kaaterskill High Peak and Round Top.

While North Point was widely known and visited during the hotel days of the nineteenth century, it was not as popular as the lower ledges and lookouts that have been memorialized by the painters of the Hudson River School: Thomas Cole (Catskill Mountain House), Sanford R. Gifford (Catskill Mountains), W. H. Bartlett (The Two Lakes and the Mountain House in the Catskills), and others both renowned and anonymous.

A selection of prints and a detailed history of the area may be studied in Roland Van Zandt's classic, *The Catskill Mountain House*. Van Zandt expresses his own opinion that the trails in this vicinity are "some of the most beautiful of the Atlantic Seaboard."

Leave North Point on the blue trail you came up on, reaching the trail junction of

The ledges of Pine Orchard

the Mary's Glen and Escarpment Trails within ten minutes. Turn left on the blue trail into a flat walk through birch and hemlock woods with occasional thick spruce and laurel appearing. You will traverse large, flat rocks and blueberry patches in this arboreous, gardenlike section of trail, with views to the east as it passes in and out of pure scrub spruce stands. In ten minutes you will reach a large, flat, stony area with views of Round Top, Kaaterskill High Peak, and the river valley to the east. Now the trail descends into forest, where large rock overhangs will eventually bring you to Badman Cave (also a shallow overhang) and the Rock Shelter Trail Junction (yellow), alongside a small wetland. Follow left on the blue trail, over a rocky surface with far-reaching views southward, descend suddenly into a marshy area, and continue to Newmans Ledge, a dangerous vertical wall of a hundred feet or more.

Be cautious, but watch for gliding birds of prey here as you gaze below into Rip Van Winkle Hollow. Look carefully and you might see the Old Mountain Road against the north face of the hollow. A wide view of the valley greets you here, and some varied initials and graffiti on the rocks.

Continue along the escarpment's edge and into the forest for twenty minutes and you'll reach the yellow spur (left) to Sunset Rock. By all means take this dead-end walk of ten minutes, for it leads to perhaps the most scenic lookout in the erstwhile domain of the Catskill Mountain House, if not in the Catskills themselves.

The many ledges around Sunset Rock and Artists Rock, the latter lying ahead, were the popular viewpoints from which scenes of the Mountain House were painted in the highly romanticized fashion typical of their admirers. Thomas Cole could see his home in Catskill from these points, and he would show it to friends from the area around Artists Rock.

The youthful and daring may want to slide back down to the trail anywhere possible to avoid backtracking, or look around for the Bear's Den route, a cavernous tunnel that reaches the trail below. The sharp drop off the south end of Sunset Rock was once the location of Jacob's Ladder, a long wooden ladder removed by the DEC as a safety precaution. If in doubt, return the way you came.

At the trail junction, turn left and continue south past the long wall of conglomerates of which Sunset Rock is made, wind around in front of the rock wall, and you will reach Artists Rock within five minutes. Another ledge follows in this fairytale forest of flat rock and pine trees that long ago earned the area the name Pine Orchard, which extended to the ledges around the Mountain House.

The trail will drop down into the campground picnic area and bathing beach at this point, where bathroom facilities and telephone are available. Turn right and walk the half-mile back to your car at Mary's Glen.

To learn more about the area, stop and browse at the Haines Falls Library, which is on your left on O'Hara Road just before it joins NY 23A.

Hunter Mountain

Distance: 6.7 miles (add 2 for Colonel's Chair)
Time: 7 hours
Vertical rise: 2,240 feet
Map: NY–NJTC Catskill Trails Map #41

Hunter is a big mountain that is best hiked on the long, gradual trail from Spruceton. The considerable vertical rise of 2,240 feet is distributed evenly over the trail so that it is never too steep from this western approach. The trails from Stony Clove Notch, although interesting and more direct, are shorter and steeper, best reserved for more aggressive hikers or for days when you are more in the mood for an assault rather than a pleasant day's outing.

Driving east on NY 23A from Grand Gorge turn south on NY 42 at Lexington. After 4.2 miles turn left on County Route 6. From the south, NY 42 is reached conveniently by NY 28 out of Kingston, and from Catskill by NY 23 or NY 23A. County Route 6, Spruceton Road, which leads to the trail, takes you through a very attractive upper-elevation flatland with a high-plains character, surrounded by the peaks of North Dome (3,610 feet), West Kill (3,880 feet), Rusk (3,680 feet), and Hunter. Trout fishing is good in the West Kill Creek. Drive past the trail to West Kill Mountain, which will appear on your right at three miles, and continue for another three miles into the Forest Preserve access parking area, where there are several trail signs. Locate the blue

trail on the road's north side, which leads to the John Robb lean-to, Hunter Mountain, Devil's Tombstone Campsite, and Platte Clove Mountain Road.

Setting out along a well-defined truck trail, you follow what was once the Jones Gap Turnpike, which was built in the late nineteenth century. The road was later improved to build and maintain the Hunter Mountain fire tower, and it is still in good enough shape to be driven by four-wheel drive vehicles (which are not allowed). After a half-mile the trail turns east and steepens gradually. Forty minutes into the hike you arrive in the saddle between Rush and Hunter Mountains, at 1.7 miles. You will see an unmarked trail leading downhill to the north through Taylor Hollow, which is no longer state-marked or maintained. This section of the old Hunter Road leads to South Jewett on NY 23A, west of the village of Hunter. Although it still exists, and may appear on older topographic maps, it is not marked and is very difficult to find from NY 23A.

Your trail continues east from here, uphill, reaching a good spring on the right within a half-mile. Near the spring, views to the north and southwest are good, with Rusk and West Kill in the foreground. The John Robb lean-to is ahead 0.1 mile on your left at the 3,500-foot mark.

Continue for another mile into a flat area of thick evergreens, and you come upon the Colonel's Chair Trail, which branches north following yellow markers. This is part of the old Shanty Hollow Trail, which is no longer in use below Colonel's Chair, having been erased by ski trail construction. It is still possible, however, to hike out from the summit lodge directly into the town of Hunter if you want, by following the ski trails.

The mile-long side trip to Colonel's Chair and the ski lifts and summit lodge of the Hunter Mountain Ski Area is worth your time. Hunter's chair lift, or "Sky Ride," runs through the summer and is good to keep in mind for quick bail-out purposes (make sure to check schedules), but you'll be very far from your car. The trail descends gently into an open

The Blackhead Range from Hunter Mountain

area, with excellent views of North Mountian, High Peak and Round Top, the Blackhead Range, Onteora Mountain, and the East Jewett range, among many nameless rolling hills. At the lodge, you will see on the northwest side a trail sign showing Hunter Mountain at 2.05 miles. If you walk downhill on that trail in a northerly direction, you notice some red paint on the rocks reading "Lookout Point." Here an unmarked and vague trail leads a short way down to a rocky ledge with more of the same impressive views. The Colonel's Chair, so called for its shape, is named for Colonel William Edwards, an early "tanlord" after whom Edwardsville was first named. The village name later changed to Hunter.

There are picnic tables at the summit lodge, and there are refreshments, food,

and communications available year-round. To the south, another 1,000 feet in elevation, you can see the fire tower near Hunter's summit.

After you return to the blue trail, the summit is a mile along the trail to your left. The heavily rutted trail leads you through a dense forest of spruce and fir with occasional ledges and views to the northeast. From the Colonel's Chair Trail it will take you about forty minutes to walk to the summit. Once you have looked around on this rocky peak and have enjoyed the 360-degree view from its fire tower, by all means continue on the blue trail to the "true summit," where the fire tower and lean-to previously were located. This additional distance takes about ten minutes and is worth the little extra effort. When you reach the old tower site, where the Becker Hollow Trail descends very steeply into Stony Clove, you see a forest of evergreens with some evidence of camping debris strewn about. Go west, a short way through this forest, and you will discover a west-facing ledge that is very private and has excellent views from the north-northwest to the south-southwest, including West Kill, North Dome, Sherrill, Balsam, Vly, Bearpen, and many lesser peaks. This is the place to rest, have lunch, and escape detection.

Longstreth, whose 1918 guide is considered a classic account of Catskill Mountain trails, sums up Hunter's view aptly: "Hunter is a climb-repaying mountain. From the steel tower on the top the entire Catskill mountainland is visible. Stony Clove, the cross-bar of the letter 'H,' which is completed by the valleys of the Esopus and the Schoharie, is but a gash in mother earth. The mass of the southern Catskills rises in ranged domes, which on that morning dropped into gulfs made pearl gray by the mists of melting snow. Westward the chain that walls the valley toward Lexington wandered away until it grew soft with lilacs and lavendars (sic)." He suggests that "if you have your nerve with you, climb Hunter some forenoon that promises thunder . . . nowhere else can you find more beautiful concentrations of vapor."

Looking east along the Devil's Path, Longstreth couldn't help commenting on the visual boisterousness of the place. If you do fall prey to a thunderstorm at this elevation, your quickest escape is Becker Hollow, which if you haven't arranged for a shuttle would leave only the devil to pay. A better bet for immediate shelter is the lean-to at Devil's Acre, 1.25 miles south on the yellow trail. A good water source is located there. Better yet, to assure your full appreciation of any Catskill peak, hike only on clear days with plenty of sunshine.

Hunter Mountain is the second highest peak in the Catskills. For a long time it was thought to be the highest, until Arnold Guyot, a Princeton geologist, proved otherwise. It was annexed to the Forest Preserve in 1930 and is one of four of the Catskill 3500 Club's winter peaks. This climb is recommended for any time of the year.

From the old fire tower site you can return to Spruceton the way you came, or use the yellow trail to the Devil's Path for an interesting but longer alternative.

West Kill to Buck Ridge Lookouts

Distance: 9.6 miles
Time: 7 hours
Vertical rise: 2,000 feet
Map: NY–NJTC Catskill Trails Map #41

This is the longer but gentler approach to West Kill from Spruceton. Although the elevation gain is considerable at 2000 feet, representing more of a vertical climb than the trail from the eastern end of Spruceton Road (1780-foot rise), the ascent is more broken up and not such a workout. Also, if you already have hiked Diamond Notch to West Kill Falls, you will have seen the only reason to come in from the east (the falls) and will enjoy more new country on the western approach.

To reach the trailhead, turn left off NY 23A onto NY 42 in Lexington, west of Hunter. Follow 42 toward Shandaken into West Kill. About 4.2 miles from 23A you will see signs for Spruceton on County Route 6. Turn left here, and go 3.7 miles to the West Kill Summit trail, which you'll see on your right. This is the extreme west end of the Devil's Path Trail (red), which also leads to Diamond Notch Lean-to, the Spruceton–Old Hunter Road, Devil's Acre Lean-to, the Hunter Mountain Fire Tower, and Devil's Tombstone, on NY 214.

Go immediately uphill through a hardwood and pine forest. The trail levels out shortly, suddenly turning right instead of following an overgrown jeep road that

leads straight ahead. After ten minutes you find that you are walking the border of a forest transition, with hemlock on your right and hardwood on your left. To your right is Mink Hollow (not to be confused with the better-known Mink Hollow near Lake Hill) and its brook, which joins the West Kill. Large boulders covered in moss decorate the forest. Grouse may burst from dense cover as you walk along.

After twenty minutes or so over rocky, root-covered footing, you meet the creek that runs into Mink Hollow. The trail then veers left, ascending into a rocky hardwood forest. In ten minutes you hear a spring bubbling beneath the trail, as you look ahead into a gap or opening in the forest where a dry pond (seasonal) sits between West Kill and North Dome. The gap runs south into the head of Broadstreet Hollow and the two ponds designated as Camp Timberlake on your map.

There are two signs at this pond section on the trail, one indicating West Kill Mountain summit at 3.01 (it's safe to assume this is intended to mean 3.1). The other shows Spruceton Road as back the way you came.

Turn sharply uphill to the north. Continue climbing for twenty minutes or more, over the steepest section of trail you will encounter. The trail eases over grassy, fern-covered flats through ledges and undulating terrain where beech and cherry appear. This pattern continues for another twenty minutes until you descend more steeply than you'd like to. But the drop is not severe or prolonged; it flattens out and the trail climbs again momentarily. Be very careful here while negotiating the slanted slabs of bluestone that the trail crosses. When wet they can be as slippery as ice.

As you ascend to a level walk again, it will take you twenty more minutes through winding flats to climb finally into alpine terrain where the trail narrows and balsam becomes prolific. At this point, no sooner do you realize you are on a summit ridge, than a sign noting West Kill Summit appears on your right, above a set of stones arranged as a crude campfire ring. You will begin to wonder where the view is—but there is none from West Kill Summit.

Continue for another three to five min-utes, to the ledge of Buck Ridge. This is a view often on the favorite list of hikers, and it is impressive. There is enough room for a dozen people to rest here, poised in midair looking at a 180-degree collection of peaks. From left to right you can see Windham, Thomas Cole, Black Dome, Blackhead, Hunter West with its ski trails, Hunter and its fire tower, West Hunter, Plateau, Overlook and its fire tower (for Hawkeyes only), Slide, Table, Lone, Rocky Peak, Wittenberg, Cornell, Friday, Balsam Cap, Ashokan High Point, the Mohonk Preserve, a piece of the Ashokan Reservoir, and down into Lanesville on NY 214. You can also see a widening in the Hudson River, which is Vanderberg Cove, as well as Olderbark, Little Rocky, Carl Mountain (in the fore-ground), and Mount Tremper to the right of the Ashokan Reservoir. See if you can find its fire tower.

Before you leave the summit, to retrace your steps, you may want to collect some balm of Gilead—the pitch of bal-sam fir—to save in a film container. This resin from the blisters of balsam is said to have medicinal value; it does keep bacteria and fungi to a minimum, at least in the tree's case. People once thought that it must also do that for them, recalling the prophet Jeremiah's reference to the balm that ancient Israelites found on Mount Gilead in the Holy Land. Indians called the balsam *cho-koh-tung*, or "biisters." The resin was used commercially to create adhesives for lenses and microscope slides until synthetics were found to be superior.

About the only thing you'll want to do with balm of Gilead is stash it in with your Christmas ornaments or keep it in a desk drawer as a freshener. Use it to whiff that nostalgic thrill of the holidays, or to return to West Kill summit during times when life's requirements don't let you do so.

West Kill Mountain

Diamond Notch to West Kill Falls

Distance: 4.6 miles
Time: 3½ hours
Vertical rise: 1,500 feet
Maps: NY–NJTC Catskill Trails Map #41

This is an easy hike that takes you into Diamond Notch via an old turnpike rebuilt in 1937 as a ski and hiking trail. You begin in Lanesville on NY 214, five miles north of Phoenicia. Look for Diamond Notch Road on the left, where there are trail signs. If you come in from Hunter to the north, take NY 214 (two miles east of town), and you'll see the trail seven miles into Stony Clove, or four miles beyond Devil's Tombstone campsite, on your right. Go up Diamond Notch Road 1.1 miles to an iron bridge, cross it and park on the left. There is a better parking area 0.3 mile ahead, just beyond a house and barn, but the road washes out often, and unless you have an appropriate vehicle, you'll be better off walking.

You'll see the blue state trail markers along the trail, which follows a large stone wall on the left. Almost immediately after setting out you will discover a wide variety of wildflowers; Dutchman's-breeches, Carolina spring beauties, yellow violets, and purple trillium. You will also notice some of the yellow paint blazes of the NYS Forest Preserve. Pass by a locked steel gate where wilderness area signs appear, near an unimproved parking area and a rough campsite with scattered fire rings. Entering the trail along Hollow Tree Brook are a few over-

grown side roads, most likely logging skid roads, which you may notice as you cross a good timber bridge on stone abutments into a hardwood forest of second growth.

After fifteen minutes of hiking, just beyond the bridge, you can make out a high ridge to your left, which is part of West Kill, the ridge that forms the west side of Diamond Notch. At this point some hemlock will begin to appear, and the trail becomes heavily eroded and gullied. Soon another bridge crosses Hollow Tree Brook, and the trail begins an even ascent, continuing due north into Diamond Notch Hollow. This is most likely the spot that suggested the development of a ski trail through the notch, but you'll probably opt for the novice slopes of a sanctioned ski area after you look down from above. Look up to your left, west, and you'll see the rocky spruce-covered shoulder of West Kill's east ridge jutting out.

About 1.5 miles into the hollow you will come across a miniature waterfall on your right, and another small kill just beyond it, both running straight down the mountain, crossing the trail. If you rest here, you may get a look at the elusive hermit thrush, the shy bird that Bur-

West Kill Falls

© 1983 New York–New Jersey Trail Conference

The Catskills writes that "a man who wants to make the effort can stand today with one foot on West Kill Mountain and the other on a supporting ridge of Hunter Mountain so that he may boast ever afterward that he once stood on two mountains at the same time."* After you have enjoyed the notch and its fine view, follow the trail into an evergreen forest, descending gently to reach Diamond Notch lean-to. The shelter has a wood floor, its site is cleaner than most, and it's in good shape as far as Catskill lean-tos go. Just below the lean-to is a small wetland that contributes to the upper reaches of West Kill Creek. Follow along on what can be a fairly wet trail, with a view of Rusk Mountain ahead and slightly left. To the west of Rusk (3680 feet) is Evergreen (3360 feet) and to the east, Hunter (4040 feet), but neither summit is visible. Within fifteen minutes of the lean-to you should reach the junction with the red-marked Devil's Path Trail, and the Timber Bridge over West Kill Falls. Diamond Notch is shown at 0.7 mile back the way you came; your car is about 2.3 miles away; the nearest road is ahead on the blue trail, at one mile (Spruceton–Old Hunter Road).

The falls here are very attractive, with several tiers of ten feet or more and a succession of large pools you might want to slip into. Have a look at the ingenious porcupine-proofing around the map stand near the trail—garbage pail covers. (At this time the system is working fine.) There are good tent sites all through this area on the north side of the falls, and evidence of camping is moderate. At only a mile from the road, the area is subject to inevitable popularity and overuse—a situation not yet out of hand. You will find the falls an ideal place to picnic, camp, or spend a hot afternoon swimming. Hike out the way you came in.

roughs claimed was his favorite. Some outcroppings of thinly stratified sandstone lie ahead, hinting that the notch is not far beyond. Within five minutes there are excellent views to the southwest, highlighting (from right to left) Slide, Table, Lone, Peekamoose, Cornell, Wittenberg, and Ashokan High Point. Up to the right is a long pile of landslide talus, with birch, cherry, and maple establishing themselves in its thin soil. Dr. Michael Kudish speculates in *Vegetational History of the Catskill High Peaks* that the slide "might date back to the 1890–1910 era when the area was logged and possibly burned."

An old road descends sharply into the ravine on the trail's west side. Now, 1.7 miles into the notch, you approach its highest point, where the mountains of West Kill and West Hunter come so close together that you can touch them both at the same time (theoretically). Alf Evers in

---

*Evers, p. 232.

Giant Ledge and Panther

Distance: 6 miles
Time: 4 hours
Vertical rise: 1,500 feet
Map: NY–NJTC Catskill Trails Map #41

This fairly easy and highly rewarding hike will take you into one of the Catskills' deepest recesses. The long ridge of Panther Mountain, which includes the lower, southerly Giant Ledge, reaches from Fox Hollow in Allaben and south to Winnisook Lake. To the east it is flanked by the extensive wilds of Woodland Valley, and to the west by Big Indian Hollow. It is here that the fledgling Esopus gains momentum, nurtured within Panther's long ridge and the western landscape with its rustic Bavarian-looking homesteads and cozy mountain hotels. Even the placenames sound rugged: Hemlock, Spruce, and Fir Mountain, Eagle Mountain Road, Elk Brook, Lost Clove, Big Indian. As you drive in from Big Indian you will begin to feel why this valley was the birthplace of legends.

The most famous legend, many versions of which have emerged as happens in folktelling, involves Winnisook — the Big Indian. The general plot in most versions of the legend is that Winnisook, a man over seven feet tall, fell in love with a valley farmer's daughter, who eventually rejected her husband to join Winnisook and his people. This went on for several years until Winnisook was eventually shot by Gertrude's jealous hus-

band during a typical livestock robbery; the dying Indian hid within a hollow tree, where he was later discovered dead by his lover. An account from Lionel Delisser's *Picturesque Ulster* (1894) offers this summation: "Win-ni-sook was buried at the foot of the pine tree in which he had been found, Gertrude and her dusky children living near the grave until the time of her death."

Still other versions of the legend maintain that Winnisook became a civilized farmer who was overcome by wolves. In his memory, local farmers carved his statue from a large tree, which stood near the site of his death. No matter which interpretation is embraced, and there are many to choose from, the active imagination will find such events to be plausible, as they are tame in proportion to the obvious fantasy of many period legends. When you consider the history of the Catskills' early wars, pioneer expansion, and frequent confrontations between Indians and settlers, the tale is even more enticing. Make up a few paragraphs of your own while you hike into Giant Ledge.

Turn south at Big Indian off of NY 28 and on to County Route 47 between Shandaken and Pine Hill, and go 7.3

miles to the hairpin turn on the way to the Slide Mountain trailhead. At the hairpin there is a large parking area on your right. The trail to Giant Ledge begins across the road on your left. It follows the yellow Phoenicia–East Branch Trail first, intersecting with the Giant Ledge–Panther–Fox Hollow Trail (blue) in a littler more than one half-mile.

The hike to Giant Ledge is 1.3 miles. This initial section goes uphill over a rough and rocky trail, crosses a dry streambed (seasonal), and again ascends through a hardwood forest and into some large sedimentary rock gardens. The hike

to the blue trail junction will take no more than a half-hour, when you will reach a long flat walk with an unmaintained, unauthorized trail going right and downhill onto the private lands of the Winnisook Club. Turn left, and within a stone's throw you will be at the triple-trail junction where the Phoenicia–East Branch Trail joins the blue trail to Giant Ledge.

Continue toward Giant Ledge Lean-to (0.85 mile). There is no designation or mileage listed for Giant Ledge itself, which actually is not a single identifiable site but consists of a long ridge above the lean-to, which is well-kept and clean. A nearby spring and the lean-to's proximity to Giant Ledge make this an attractive camping spot.

Once upon the ledge, or series of ledges, pick a vacant vantage point (this is a very popular spot) on the east side. You will be looking toward Fork Ridge and into Woodland Valley, with Terrace, Cornell, and Wittenberg to your right (southwest). To the northeast you will be able to identify the lower peaks of Garfield and Sheridan, with Romer to the east and Tremper beyond it, including various members of the Devil's Path Range from northeast to east. On the west side of Giant Ledge, several open rocks make possible views of Hemlock, Spruce, Fir, Big Indian, Eagle, Haynes, Balsam, and Belleayre Mountains. There are many isolated outlooks all over the ridge here, so take some time to poke around and explore the many footpaths that run from east to west, leading to additional viewpoints. The ledge is predominantly scrub hardwood covered, but at its north end there is a virgin spruce grove, which you'll see extending to the ledge's base.

You'll have more time to explore the ledge on your return from Panther, which is another 1.75 miles beyond the ledge and an additional 500 feet in elevation. This takes you another forty minutes of hiking, going slightly downhill at first and then climbing vigorously through large boulders and thick hardwood forest, passing a spring on the right. You have several views of Slide, Wittenberg, and Cornell as you cross open rock terraces.

The Panther summit is an expanded version of Giant Ledge in terms of views and topography, with isolated openings in the dense coniferous forest — yielding views of the Panther Kill Valley, Fork Ridge, and the village of Phoenicia with its two bridges crossing the Esopus. While the ledges on Panther face mostly to the east, some face west, and you can even look around for northerly views of Sheridan, Garfield, North Dome, Sherrill, and Balsam.

On the north side of Panther, the trail (completed in 1936) descends into Fox Hollow over a jeep trail that would make an attractive cross-country ski run, suggesting that this could be an adventurous two-car loop if you had skiing in mind. The loop ups the trip mileage to seven total, about three of which can be skied if conditions are powdery. There are some breakneck sections where walking would be advisable.

From the summit of Panther you are an easy 1.75 miles from Giant Ledge and another 1.25 miles from your car.

Giant Ledge Trailhead

Wittenberg and Cornell

Distance: 7 miles
Time: 5 hours
Vertical rise: 2,480 feet
Map: NY–NJTC Catskill Trails Map #43

Wittenberg (3780 feet) is a favorite among local hikers, who praise it as one of the Catskills' most dramatic. Although not panoramic, the view encompasses an impressive 180-degree hemisphere of mountain and valley that reaches north over the Devil's Path Range and the escarpment, east over the Hudson and Taconics, and south over an extended variety of terrain where the Gunks taper off into endless flatlands. It is in many ways similar to the escarpment view of Pine Orchard fame, the single most lauded overlook in Catskill history. It offers intimate observation of the nearby peaks stretching from Peekamoose to Friday and in its eastern lowlands the Ashokan Reservoir, which is almost entirely visible.

The scene impressed John Burroughs, who visited there after a "long and desperate" attempt at Slide: "The view from the Wittenberg is in many respects more striking, as you are perched immediately above a broader and more distant sweep of country, and are only about 200 feet lower. You are here on the eastern brink of the lower Catskills, and the earth falls away at your feet and curves through an immense stretch of forest until it joins the plain of Shokan, and thence sweeps away to the Hudson and beyond."

The "plain of Shokan" is now the site of the Ashokan Reservoir, which is impounded in 1913 to supply water for New York City. Ashokan is Iroquois, meaning "place of fish." Slide is not visible from where Burroughs stood, but it is included in a collection of good views on the western side, along the trail to Cornell.

To reach the trailhead at Woodland Valley State Campground, take Woodland Valley Road, which you'll see on the left, 0.7 mile west of Phoenicia on NY 28. After crossing the Esopus Creek, turn right and continue along this road until you reach the state campground at 4.9 miles.

Woodland Valley is one of the Catskills' deepest and most romantic valleys. A hideaway for recluse, hiker, and flyfisher, it penetrates into the park's most remote peaks. You'll enjoy the sense of rugged terrain, the intriguing architecture of valley homesteads, and the lively creeks of Panther Kill and Dougherty Brook.

Do not rely on topo maps and earlier guidebooks, which place this trail a mile back to the east, where a suspended bridge led the trail to Terrace Mountain via an old bark and cross-country ski road.

From the state campground parking

area, step stones across Woodland Valley Creek, on the road's south side. Find the red trail, which is well-defined and marked. Don't be disheartened by the immediate ascent involved in this 3.4 mile hike to the summit of Wittenberg; the rise eases considerably, before steepening again as the summit is approached. Proceed through a heavily forested and boulder-strewn grove of large hemlock and maple trees. The trail is well-marked here, but because of its many boulders, it is not self-guiding. So keep a close eye on the markers as you boulder-hop, or it will be easy to stray off the trail. As the forest type changes subtly into mixed hardwood, footing eases into occasional flat walks through high ledgy terrain and frequent dark stands of hemlock. After a half hour's hike the trail becomes predominantly self-guiding and remains so until you encounter more rock in the upper elevations.

After an hour of moderate effort, allowing for observation, refreshment, or photographing, you'll reach a trail junction, where you turn right for the 1.1-mile Wittenberg climb. The ascent is characterized by attractive (albeit steep) terraces, unusual rock formations, and penetrating vertical crevices. The forest cover will have changed notably into spruce and fir, and as Kudish in *Vegetational History of the Catskill High Peaks*, comments, "On even slopes the transition from slope to ridge forests is gradual and barely noticeable to the observer. But just as frequently, however, a high ledge will create an abrupt break in the topography, creating a likewise abrupt break in the forest. Examples of such rapid transitions from slope to ridge forest occur at the north slope of Wittenberg at 3000 feet along the trail."

Within thirty minutes of diligent stalking you will have bagged the summit, which includes an intriguing array of sheltered outcroppings and open ledges facing

© 1983 New York–New Jersey Trail Conference

east. There is evidence of illegal camping (above 3500 feet) in the surrounding forest, which, however, does not detract from your aesthetic appreciation of the place. Although the profusion of mosses, lichens, and various forest cover is typical of Catskill peaks, it is interesting to note the absence of alpine species. Kudish speculates that these could have been eliminated by the trampling of hikers. Below the summit ledge a short distance is a large overhang that may be convenient in the event of rain.

After lunching and resting on the Wittenberg, you will want to observe some westerly views, which can be done best by hiking the short trail to Cornell via the

View of the Devil's Path from Wittenberg

ridge that connects them, a narrow and interesting rock path that is several feet wide. Cornell's westerly shoulder provides a good view of the slide on Slide's north side, which occurred circa 1820. To see this, proceed west on the trail as if hiking to Slide. The hike to Cornell from Wittenberg is about twenty minutes. If you have arranged for a shuttle you may choose to hike Slide. If not, you must return the way you came.

This trail dates back to 1880, when John Burroughs haunted the range, relating anecdotes of the porcupines in volume six of his complete nature writings, *Riverby*. And if you've dropped your pack off on Cornell's summit to find the westerly view of Slide, don't be surprised to find the omniverous quill pig investigating your lunch when you return.

Slide Mountain

Distance: 5.6 miles
Time: 5½ hours
Vertical rise: 1,700 feet
Map: NY–NJTC Catskill Trails Map #43

Burroughs never would have suspected that the mountain that had so successfully defied his climbing efforts in the early 1880s would become one of the Catskills' most approachable high peaks. In Burroughs' time, Slide was, as he suggested, "probably the most inaccessible; certainly the hardest to get a view of, it is hedged about so completely by other peaks, the greatest mountain of them all and apparently the least willing to be seen; only at a distance of thirty or forty miles is it seen to stand up above all other peaks." Yet within a few years of Burroughs' 1885 ascent, the mountain became revealed to members of organized outings by Jim Dutcher, a bark peeler living at the foot of the mountain, who was recognized as its singular guide.

Evers tells us that "Dutcher, who kept a boardinghouse at Big Indian (Panther Mountain House) and served as the hamlet's postmaster, was among the best known of all the mountain guides and the guardian spirit of Slide Mountain."* Dutcher's trail remains to commemorate him, but today only a small section of it

is seen by hikers. The easiest way to get at Slide is from the top of Big Indian Hollow, where the Phoenicia–East Branch Trail begins within a mile of Winnisook Lake.

Take County Route 47 (Slide Mountain Road) from Big Indian Pass (heading south), pass Winnisook Lake at 8.4 miles on the left, and park at the trailhead lot a mile farther on. Don't get confused by the yellow trail that departs for Giant Ledge and Woodland Valley from the hairpin turn, before you reach Winnisook Lake. This is the same trail that goes to Slide, but it follows the road at this point. Follow the yellow markers you'll see on trees and telephone poles along the road, to the Slide Mountain parking lot.

Once afoot you immediately cross the upper reaches of the Neversink's west branch (often dry here), which flows into the Delaware River. Also originating on Slide's northwest watershed is the Esopus, which runs down through the hollow into Phoenicia, the Ashokan Reservoir, and the Hudson. Continuing on an easy uphill and heavily impacted trail through a stand of thin maple and mixed hardwood, you reach an old road that you follow to the right. When you soon reach a junction, switch to the red trail going

*Evers, p. 555.

left, where you will notice some of the stone steps that are in place at steeper sections in the trail, similar to those laid down by Dutcher in 1886.

While some current sources maintain that Dutcher's Trail was built to enable three newly appointed Forest Commissioners and a party of officials to ascend Slide in 1886 to officially designate the Catskills as a part of the State Forest Preserve, in fact the trail was developed for women. Even Burroughs commented, in a statement reflecting more the dress and cultural habits than the attitudes of his time, that the rugged and direct approach from Woodland Valley is Slide's "most difficult side," whereas from Big Indian "the climb is comparatively easy and . . . often made by women." This statement was made prior to the Dutcher Trail's appearance. From Woodland— remember that Burroughs was traversing the treacherous 1200-foot by 500-foot landslide that earned the mountain its name—he claimed that "only men can essay the ascent."

The yellow trail, by the way, follows a southwesterly course into Denning, branching off onto the Long Path that crosses Table and Peekamoose to the south, dropping sharply down into the Rondout Creek. Continuing on the red trail at a consistent twenty- to thirty-degree incline, you will notice the profusion of beech, birch, maple, and cherry. The footing is rocky but firm, and logs have been placed diagonally in some sections to minimize erosion. You will notice the red clay, which is responsible for the rapid discoloration of valley creeks during periods of heavy run-off. As you continue, you will get occasional views in southwesterly directions when the leaves are off the trees. You see subtle changes from slope to ridge forest types as you gain elevation, finally reaching a section of trail that has the character of a garden pathway.

Writers and historians have commented

Slide Mountain from Ashokan High Point

on this section of trail, taking particular notice of the presence of white quartz. Where this stratum of rock continues into Pennsylvania, it is overlaid with anthracite coal. Geologists believe that, given another 500 feet in elevation, the Catskills would have contained coal.

The history of trail locations on Slide is vast and confusing. Although some contemporary woodsmen refer offhandedly to the trail discussed here as the "old bridle path," Haring noted about 1930 that "today both [the wagon road and the bridle path] are completely abandoned, partly engulfed in landslides and at all points densly overgrown. Both are now impassable. Even the footpath follows a different route." Interestingly, Longstreth, writing about 1917, makes no remarks about either bridle path or wagon road; he was directed along a blazed trail upon which "there were no footprints." Neither does he make reference to Dutcher. Some details of his climb, i.e., "to our left the woods sloped uniformly up, on the right they fell into a ravine," and his telling of following the old telephone wire that ran to the tower, suggest an approach similar to today's.

In the "garden path" section of the Slide trail, you will be hiking in a southeasterly direction and will have several good views to the north and east. Farther ahead on the left you will reach a few outcroppings, facing east, which are positioned at the head of the landslide. The slide is not really visible from this aspect, however, and it is much more striking from a distance, as with the view from Cornell.

Shortly ahead of you a blue trail goes off to the right that runs back to the yellow trail to Denning and Peekamoose. This Curtis–Ormsbee Trail was built in 1900. From this junction, Slide is 0.65 mile ahead of you. Where the Curtis–Ormsbee Trail drops off the southwest shoulder of the mountain, a long ledge provides some good viewing and rest areas among the balsam fir. Within another half hour you reach the summit, where the best views are to the south, east, and north. There is no longer any lean-to, but evidence of camping and overuse is serious. Here is a plaque commemorating John Burroughs, which reads in part: "Here the works of man dwindle in the heart of the southern Catskills."

Slide's summit view includes nearly seventy named Catskill peaks as well as a wide view of the Hudson Valley, the Ashokan Reservoir, the Green Mountains, the Berkshires, Taconics, Hudson Highlands, and the Shawangunks. This is the same view that Commissioner Cox, climbing Slide in 1886, pronounced to be "every bit as fine as anything to be seen in the Adirondacks."

Slide was not recognized as the Catskills' highest peak until Princeton professor of geology Arnold Guyot published his map of 1879. Previously, Kaaterskill High Peak and later Hunter Mountain competed for the title in the days when a common carpenter's level was the critical measuring tool.

41

Blackhead, Black Dome, and Thomas Cole

Distance: 7 miles, 8.5 if car left at Maplecrest
Time: 6 hours
Vertical rise: 2,450 feet, cumulative
Map: NY–NJTC Catskill Trails Map #41

At the age of twenty-four, Thomas Cole, an immigrant from England, had an established reputation as a landscape painter. In 1825, in the company of a wealthy patron, Cole made a first visit to the Catskills, traveling to the House at Pine Orchard, forerunner of the fabulous Catskill Mountain House. Cole was enthralled by the views of mountains, lakes, and forests. The inspiration of those mountains played upon his nostalgic view of nature, resulting in the first major series of paintings of the mountains. The combination also firmly established Cole as a leader in the romantic realism school of painting that dominated the middle of the nineteenth century.

Cole's love of the Catskills was reflected in the paintings he made from sketches done at the scene on many trips into the mountains. His close observations of nature breathed life into his view of the romantic wilderness. He wrote of the view on the trip through the Clove near Palenville and the huge precipices above the village that "frowned over the valley like towers and battlements of cyclopean structure." He declared that the "sun shining in gleams through the tall, dark, spruce forest, upon the velvety carpet" reminded him of the

interior of some Gothic pile, where the sun comes through narrow windows in slender streams, and lights whatever it strikes with a refulgence almost supernatural, amid the gloomy shadows around."*

Although he considered the view from High Peak to be the finest in the whole Catskill Range, and spent most of his time in the mountains surrounding the Mountain House, he was impressed by the peaks in the Blackhead Range. On "an excursion to Blackhead, or the Dome Mountain as Cole loved to call it, one of the finest portions of the Catskills must always continue to be, both to the writer and the painter, one of the luminous points of the past. . . . At noon . . . the moss beneath black fir trees on the summit . . . the descent down the wooded steeps."†

It is fitting that one of the peaks in the Blackhead Range now bears Cole's name. And a hike over Blackhead, Black Dome, and Thomas Cole brings the hiker

---

*Letters from Thomas Cole, quoted in Rev. Charles Rockwell, *The Catskill Mountains and the Region Around* (Cornwall, NY: Hope Farm Press, 1973), p. 285.

†From Rockwell, p. 294.

to several vantages from which one still can share Cole's vision of wilderness without the influence of man.

A two-car shuttle is a must for this walk, which loops over the three tremendous peaks that offer the best of views in the northern Catskills. Both ends of the loop are accessible from Maplecrest, a tiny hamlet in a high valley, which boasts Maple Trees, one of the fine Catskills hotels.

Leave one car at the parking turnout at the end of Elmer Barnum Road at the west end of the valley. To find it turn south on Maple Crest Road at Maplecrest; Elmer Barnum Road is the first left. Alternatively, you can leave a car in the village, for the mile and a half downhill walk from the trailhead to the hamlet does not seem to add too much to the trip. Drive east through bucolic Black Dome Valley to a parking turnout at the end of Big Hollow Road, an extension of Maple Crest Road. Three trails depart from this trailhead. You want the southern one, which gives the distance to Black Dome as 1.8 miles; Thomas Cole, 2.5; and Elmer Barnum Road, 5.8 miles. Your walk will be 1.2 miles longer because you also will climb Blackhead.

You cross a small stream and pick up red trail markers at the registration booth. You cross and recross the Batavia Kill, beginning a gentle uphill on a broad open old road. The brook or its tributary will keep you company with charming waterfalls in spring flood. Beyond a second stream crossing, the grade increases, and in about half a mile the yellow trail to Blackhead continues straight as you turn right, still on the red trial, to follow the tributary more steeply uphill. After walking for forty minutes, you reach a spring (with pipe and safe water).

The trail is even steeper beyond and

Lunch on Black Dome looking south

Blackhead can be seen through the trees except in summer. After a fairly stiff climb, the trail levels out, and you reach a draw between Blackhead and Black Dome where a sign gives the mileage as 1.7 miles, a trip that probably took you an hour and ten minutes because of the 1,400-foot climb. Blackhead is 0.6 mile from here and so is Black Dome.

The yellow trail heads left up Blackhead, and wonderful views from this trail start almost immediately. The route is steep with stairs built into the mountainside. At the crest, the trail continues across the level top out to the narrow northeastern prong. Here is a trail intersection with the blue trail leading toward Windham High Peak and the yellow trail directly back to the valley, but you will return the way you climbed. First, walk a few feet farther to a lookout to enjoy the views across the Hudson to the Taconics. There is also a western lookout down a small path to the right of the end of the narrow prong with views of Hunter, obvious by its fire tower, across the big broad valley below.

It will take you about an hour to climb Blackhead and return to the saddle. Here, take the red trail again and immediately start to climb. Your first impression is a view back to the incredible rock mass of Blackhead. There are several scrambles and a series of ledges before you reach Black Dome's relatively level summit. That climb takes half an hour, and you will find a lovely lunch spot with views to the left of the trail, shortly after it levels out. West Kill is seen to the right of Hunter with Devil's Path and Plateau to the left of Hunter. East of Plateau lies Mink Hollow, the Sugarloaf, Indian Head, and Twin. Slide, Wittenberg, and Cornell are seen on the horizon beyond Hunter.

The trail continues across this narrow summit ridge, climbing a few ledges on the way. After about a fifteen-minute walk, you will find a second lookout, this time to the far eastern end of the range with Kaaterskill in full view. You continue across the scrubby summit with no views for another ten minutes before you begin to descend.

The long thin saddle between the peaks has been burned, and the twisted stumps give one section an other worldy air. There are views along the way, one to the west and a second toward the town of Windham and Camels Hump. You climb again, this time quite gently, to the summit of Thomas Cole, a point that is 0.7 mile from Black Dome and that, in spite of being a tribute to the famous painter, offers no views. The trail crosses the open wooded summit ridge, then begins to descend through a series of shelves and ledges, typical Catskills terrain. From the first of these knobs, you will have views of Windham and Maplecrest Valley. Below a second wooded knob, just as the trail begins a final steep descent, there are more views from an open rock ledge. The 2.65-mile, relatively level trip down from Thomas Cole to the trailhead, 1.5 miles from the hamlet, takes only an hour.

Windham High Peak Loop

Distance: 11 miles
Time: 5–7 hours
Vertical rise: 2,220 feet
Map: NY–NJTC Catskill Trails Map #41

This highly scenic and energetic hike follows the escarpment's north shoulder, with Windham High Peak forming the western height of land that reaches in an arch through the east and south. The escarpment is the sudden 2000-foot rise from the valley floor of the ridge and mountains running from Overlook and north to Windham.

From a distance the escarpment looks continuous, yet it is bisected deeply by Kaaterskill Clove (between South Mountain and Kaaterskill High Peak) and its southerly neighbor Platte Clove, between Kaaterskill High Peak and Plattekill Mountains. Otherwise, it is visually impenetrable.

The escarpment was revered by local Indians, who called it the Great Wall of Manitou. It was beyond this wall that the gods Gitchie Manitou, the spirit of good, and Mitchie Manitou, the spirit of evil, lived in eternal discord. Longfellow leaves us an interpretation of the myth: "Gitchie Manitou The Mighty."*

The Dutch settlers, who sought ground similar to the Netherland's arable flat lands, had little use for the rocky hinterland beyond the wall, as it was unsuit-

*See Haring, *Our Catskill Mountains*, p. 14.

able for farming and was still, no doubt, the devil's dwelling place. They neither strayed nor settled far beyond the river valley.

The area's beauty was spread by the genius of Irving, Cole, Bryant, Burroughs, Thoreau, Muir, and their contemporaries in art and literature. Later guidebook writers of the twentieth century, H. A. Haring in particular, described the view from the east as one of the "few places in the world where mountains stand out so impressively. . . . The rounded outlines of the range bespeak all the shadowiness and romance with which legend has clothed them, the Wall of Manitou mellows the mountains into soft contours and rounded lines that seem to flow rythmically from summit to summit."

Windham High Peak is the first "rounded outline" you will hike. Coming west on NY 23 from Catskill, turn south (left) on NY 296 to Hensonville. From there go two miles into Maplecrest on County Route 40. Turn left on County Route 56 (Big Hollow Road) until you reach Peck Road at 1.5 miles on your left. The trail begins within a mile at the end of Peck Road.

Begin on the yellow trail toward Elm Ridge lean-to (one mile), where you will also see red NYS snowmobile trail signs. Follow a dirt road through vestigial pasturelands, now grown into a forest of mixed hardwoods where stone walls mark the field divisions of early settlements. A side trail will branch off to your right into an evergreen stand. Avoid it, continuing on yellow markers. In fifteen minutes you should reach the trail junction and the blue (Escarpment Trail) markers indicating Windham High Peak, Burnt Knob, and Acra Point to the right. The Elm Ridge lean-to will appear on your right as you continue. The lean-to is well situated and frequently used. Nearby campsites are plentiful, however, if you are interested in spending the night. One good spot in particular is located on a spur trail (yellow) that leads left (north) off the blue trail just above the lean-to. It provides a good view to the north-northwest.

After a half hour of hiking, about one mile from your starting point, you pass through some thick, dark evergreen forests that will spark your imagination. This stretch used to be quite wet in early season, but has been recently improved by AMC. The trail then bends gently through hardwood, gradually ascending.

When you reach the southerly shoulder of the mountain at 3000 feet in elevation, you will get a look at the nearby Blackhead Range and the more westerly East Jewett Range. At this point, you are two miles into the walk and will turn northeast for the half-mile, 520-foot climb to the summit. During periods of scanty foliage in this birch, cherry, and maple forest, you will be able to look east at Burnt Knob and Acra Point and the long escarpment ridge. The last incline will take you about thirty minutes. Once on the long, level summit, you will discover a

Windham High Peak

benchmark and some remarkable views.

The most imposing of these will be into the Blackhead Range, which feels remarkably close. Down and to your right, or southwest, you will see the sister peaks of Round (2585 feet) and Van Loan Hill (2500 feet). The westerly views are off to the northwest side of the summit, on a short spur to a rocky area that you will find easily. From this point you see a long line of lesser peaks disappearing into the Schoharie Valley, including Ginseng, Zoar, and Cave Mountain, and slightly to the north, Richmond and Huntersfield Mountains with Ashland Pinnacle between them. You can also see the Windham ski area.

The most popular view is from beyond the summit, east, where a graffiti-inscribed outcropping hangs above the Hudson Valley. (These inscriptions are not of the same genre as the North Lake variety, and the few decent initials have been heavily eroded and defaced with the deep and careless scrawls of heavy chisels.) From here you can see the Helderberg escarpment and, on a clear day, Albany. It is also likely that you'll see Vermont's Green Mountains, the Berkshires, and the Taconic Range. Looking down over the ridge you'll see Burnt Knob (3180 feet), the second knoll from Windham Peak. The precise position of Acra Point is not discernible from here, as it follows a long and fairly level ridgeline around to the east.

Leave the summit, going steeply downhill through hardwood, reaching the scenic col between Windham High Peak and Burnt Knob in thirty-five minutes or so. The views are similar to those looking south from Windham High Peak, although you are lower and closer to the valley views. Watch for occasional yellow-marked spurs that lead to views. Continue up Burnt Knob, which you will scale in another half hour or so, where more views look both north and south on varia-

tions of Black Dome Valley and the expanse of northern lowlands.

You then descend into the 2800-foot saddle between Burnt Knob and Acra Point, where the red Black Dome Range Trail intersects the Escarpment Trail. If you wish to shorten your hike back to Peck Road via Big Hollow Road, this is the place to do it. If not, continue uphill, gaining several hundred feet of elevation before reaching Acra Point after twenty-five minutes. Views from the Point are limited to the north and south, more of a wider perspective of the valley view toward Hensonville.

All along the ridge from Burnt Knob through Acra Point and south to the junction of the Escarpment and Batavia Kill Trails (yellow) there are crude campsites and campfire rings constructed among the balsam. As you travel south from Acra Point they become bigger, more conspicuous, and more frequent, commanding narrow overlooks with restricted views to the east. There are no views to the west along this ridge, which will take perhaps an hour to hike. At some points you will be able to peer down the escarpment to the south. The Blackheads will be visible periodically also, ahead through the trees. If the yellow Batavia Kill Trail seems long in coming, don't worry; it's hard to miss it. You will descend nearly 200 feet (in 0.5 mile) to reach the junction, where you turn right and drop another 200 feet to the Batavia Kill Lean-to, which is no more than ten minutes beyond the junction.

Hike out, picking up the red Black Dome Range Trail, which comes in on your left within fifteen minutes. Here, two creeks converge. You are now only a half-mile from the road, and you must walk it back to Peck Road unless you've arranged for a shuttle or can talk someone into giving you a ride—which by now your feet will appreciate.

Western
Catskills

Delaware County Trails—East

Distance: 9.9 miles
Time: 6 hours
Vertical rise: 2,200 feet cumulative
Map: NY–NJTC Catskill Trails Map #44

If the western parts of Delaware County's trails sparkle in spring, the eastern ones are best enjoyed in the warm glow of autumn. These ridges often open up to reveal views of the long narrow valleys of the western Catskills. Falling leaves reveal even more vistas of the eroded peneplain, its gentle hills draped in reds, golds, and russets. And early fall, while the leaves are still falling, occurs before deer hunting season, a time all hikers avoid.

Another charm of the western Catskills is its network of back roads that wind in and out of valleys, along streams, and past charming hamlets, in a maze that demands a good map. More than a good map will be needed to spot cars at the two ends of this through walk. From Exit 96 of NY 17 at Livingston Manor, take Debruce Road south 0.8 mile to Old Route 17 (also County Route 178 and 179). In 1.8 miles turn right toward Beaverkill on County Route 151. A left turn at 6.2 miles is marked Beaverkill Campsite. The campsite, at 6.8 miles, is beside the Beaverkill and its historic covered bridge. Cross the bridge and bear

Passing bluestone ledges on Mary Smith Hill

left on Berry Brook Road for 1.2 miles until it intersects Holiday Road (a sharp left fork toward Roscoe). Here you bear right on Holiday and Berry Brook Road, past a small grass airstrip, past Henderson Hollow Road, to a parking turnout on the right side of the road, 4.8 miles from the bridge. Spot one car here and return past the Beaverkill to County Route 151 where you will turn left for 3.1 miles to Lew Beach. On the way, County Route 151 becomes 152. Soon after entering Ulster County, the route number changes again to County Route 54, which you will follow for 3.8 more miles to a left fork toward Little Pond Campsite, which is under a mile down the access road.

It is wise to notice the turns carefully—late in the day when you are winding back to retrieve one car here, the roads all will seem quite different.

The hike begins at Little Pond Campsite, and directions for the walk are much simpler than those for the trailheads. From the parking area beside the pond a trail heads up Touchmenot Mountain, a viewless peak that this trip avoids. Instead, follow the shore—either side will do—and pick up yellow markers as the trail leads past many lovely campsites. If you are following the right or east side, you cross an inlet and near campsite 70 a right fork leads you onto the Little Trout Pond Trail, away from the lake. It follows a hemlock- and spruce-filled gorge and passes not far from a marsh with views of Touchmenot Mountain. Just beyond, the trail intersects an old roadway and turns right to follow it uphill through a field. After passing through a reforestation area, the trail enters a larger open field, where a triple marker alerts you to the fact that there are no markers in the field, the scattered apple trees being too infrequent to mark the route. Go straight ahead and cross the field to reach another old roadway, which the trail follows right, north into a series of open fields with stone walls and gorgeous views of Beaverkill Valley.

The route continues up past the last field through scrub forests to intersect the red-marked Touchmenot Trail, after a forty-five-minute 1.6-mile walk. The way right comes from Touchmenot Mountain;

you turn left, on a much less well-traveled route.

The trail is narrow and winding, often hard to follow as it turns toward Cabot Mountain. You will scramble up a cliff of bluestone and angle right along the ridge top. The route is typically Catskill, sharp thrusts up ledges, then short levels. A second ridge just short of Cabot's 2,970-foot summit and another short climb lead to a left fork, which ends in fifty feet at a viewpoint over Little Pond, about a half hour's walk from the intersection.

If you return to the trail, you can continue across Cabot's small flat top, then begin to descend. Again the way is down a ledge, then across a level, and down once more. Some of the levels are handsome with evergreen woodfern and bluestone boulders beneath the scrub oak and maple. After a thirty-minute-walk from the viewpoint, you find you are descending quite steeply into the valley of Beech Hill Brook, which flows north, and a tributary of the Beaverkill, which flows south from the saddle. As you reach the saddle, you find the trail occupies a narrow access piece of state land between two posted parcels. An hour and a half walk past the intersection, 2.75 miles, you emerge on Beech Hill Road, a macadam surface, and head north, right, along it for a quarter mile. Here a guideboard on the left side of the road directs you 0.9 mile to Middle Mountain Vista, two miles to Mary Smith Road, and 5.3 miles to Holiday Brook Road.

In a hundred yards or so, the road you are following leads to a quarry and through it into the woods. Just before a gate on the road, 150 feet from the quarry, the trail heads steeply left uphill. After the first sharp thrust, the route again climbs a series of ledges, with the levels here filled with brambles and blackberries. The first ledge you reach is viewless, but the following descent and short climb bring you to a second knob, which offers a view over the gentle hills that border Mary Smith Hill Valley. Do not be surprised if it takes you fifty minutes to traverse the stated 0.9 mile to the vista, for the real distance is somewhat more.

Beyond, you climb a bit, to the long level mountaintop, then descend to briefly follow the ridgetop before angling left for a traverse of the steep, almost cliffy mountain side. The trail is rubble-filled with bluestone, not easy walking. As the trail levels out into a parklike open area, you sense the deep valley on your right. The long traverse leads you to the saddle between the two hills, and as you approach it you catch a glimpse of the next peak you will climb. You may feel a valley opening out on your left as well, as you follow a stone wall that leads you to a dirt road. About forty-five minutes is required for the descent from the vista spot.

Your destination, Holiday Brook Road, is now 3.3 miles away, over the top of Mary Smith Hill. The trail quickly starts up that hill through a reforestation area, a reprise of the previous hills with sharp climbs and short levels. Scarcely fifteen minutes takes you to a view of the hills to the south. You continue to traverse the left side of the hilltop with steep cliffs below, reaching another view spot in about ten minutes. Here you look over the valley of Mary Smith Hill Road toward the hamlet of Lew Beach.

The continuing route is down into a small swale filled with mountain wood fern as well as the evergreen wood fern. You follow a lovely long ridge lush with ferns, crossing to the right or north side of the mountain, then back to the south side to climb a last ridge. In spite of the dense forest, you are aware of the valley almost vertically below. The trail angles left along the scarp through brambles, then down to a point with a through-the-trees view. Beyond, you descend a cut, then traverse back right. The next section of trail demands rerouting. It is sufficiently steep and rubbly as to make treacherous footing. Finally, about an hour and fifty minutes from Mary Smith Hill Road, you reach a level field and quickly emerge beside the parking area on Holiday Brook Road.

Delaware County Trails—West

Distance: 12.5 miles
Time: 7 hours
Vertical rise: 2,350 feet cumulative
Map: NY–NJTC Catskill Trails Map #44

Spring wildflowers beckon. Find friends to share this long walk through the Delaware County hills; for spotting a car at either end makes a through trip possible. The trails are easily accessible from NY 17; take it to NY 206 west across the Beaverkill to a left turn onto Morton Hill Road, then left again on Russell Brook Road (which may be unmarked). This narrow dirt road winds by the lovely gorge of Russell Brook and brings you to a pullout in 2.9 miles from NY 206. Here you can leave one car.

Return to NY 206, Cat Hollow Road. Turn west across the Beaverkill, and continue for 3.6 miles to Little Spring Brook Road, a right turn. Follow the road 1.1 miles to the end, and park on the side of the road away from private driveways. The marked trailhead is just ahead.

You start by continuing on Little Spring Brook Road, which bears yellow markers, and a sign pointing ahead 0.6 mile to the fork of Pelnor Hollow and Campbell Mountain trails, 1.4 miles to Mary Smith Trail, 3.7 miles to Pelnor Hollow lean-to, and 6 miles to Campbell Mountain lean-to.

If you have timed this right—midMay is best—the walk through third-growth forest is quickly livened by crinkle-root in

bloom. A lovely old stone fence borders the way. You walk beside a beaver flow that has flooded part of the trail, looking at anemones and wild oats. Continue up a gentle hill through taller forest stands to an intersection. The yellow trail forks right to Berry Brook Road, you go straight on the blue trail, which also bears snowmobile trail markers. The guideboard gives the distance of your destination at Russell Brook Road as 11.9 miles. Apple trees in the clearing and Norway spruce mark the lovely old settlement spot. Scenes like this were once the site of Burrough's hourglass trees. You still see a few, driving past the dairy pastures of Delaware County; these red thorn trees of the hawthorne family were sculpted into hourglasses as the cattle foraged their persistent shoots, which finally extended into a large enough circle to protect a central stem from which emerged the tree, formed like the top of an hourglass.

The trail continues beside lovely old rock walls through a reforestation area, and quickly forks left through the stone wall into that forest. Mayflowers, twisted stalk, painted trillium, and spring beauties are all in bloom as you contour around the hillside on a narrow trail through a beautiful, high, open forest. Dwarf ginseng and a carpet of white violets and spring beauties edge the trail.

After about an hour of walking you will find the trail crosses an intermittent stream and shortly after crosses an old woods road. Your trail angles left, following a portion of road, then leaves the road and the snowmobile trail where double blue markers indicate a right, up-hill, turn. You are on the gentle approach to the eastern of Brock Mountain's two summits. A few minutes along the trail, almost beside a great gray whale created from the linear faulting on a huge erratic bluestone boulder, you make a sharp left turn to continue uphill. The way is through a berry patch, then a swamp where the trail seems obscured, but a view of the small summit, about 150 feet higher, points the way. Watch for trout lilies on the continuing climb. As the summit levels out, you can see through the trees the outline of a portion of Pepacton Reservoir.

The trail starts down, gently at first, then more steeply, until you reach a roadway. Turn right on it, and after a hundred yards turn left on a narrow path across the Brock's small northern summit, west of which you pass a slag heap from a bluestone quarry. These small quarries were neither as famous nor as extensive as those in Ulster County, especially the one at West Hurley, now buried beneath the Ashokan Reservoir. Still, in the nineteenth century, before cement made quarrying unprofitable, many such small quarries were opened in the Catskills. The bluestone, a fine, compacted sandstone, often quite blue, but in varying shades of gray and green as well, was quarried in uncounted small pits. After the overburden of soil and trees was removed and roads for stone sledges built to the sites, the quarrymen gambled that the stone would split into the large, flat layers for which the rock was famous. H. A. Haring in his history, *Our Catskill Mountains*, said that "all through these mountains the abandoned workings of these quarries tell a tragic tale. . . . Few quarrymen were able to retain the great profits they made in this business." As quarrymen strove to open more and more pits to increase their earnings, often the rock, instead of splitting into sidewalk slabs, crumbled into waste that is now visible in many tailings pits.

Angling left, again following a roadway, you begin the long, gentle downhill that affords a limited view across the valley to Campbell Mountain, the next peak on this day's walk. The roadway, undoubtedly used by horses to drag stone-boats downhill, never uphill, is steeper than you would expect an old woods road to be. Many, like this one, as Haring noted, are "so precipitous . . . that even the hiker of today prides himself that he is able to scramble up or down, and visitors regularly question that these 'roads' were ever used by teams at all."

As the old road begins to descend more steeply, you may hear road sounds from the highway below. You continue downhill for twenty minutes more, passing stone fences and old fieldstone foundations. After two hours and twenty minutes, you emerge on NY 206, having completed 4.7 miles of the walk.

Across the road and down to the left, a sign gives Russell Brook Road as 7.8 miles distant and the Trout Pond Trail as 2.4 miles away. The way down toward a deep valley leads quickly across a stream in a lovely little spruce glen with an interesting old foundation. A few feet farther, on the right, stop and examine the beautiful stonework of another abandoned farmsite.

Beyond a bridge that takes you over Cat Hollow Brook, you angle left, uphill, to follow yet another old woods road. The road goes straight at the point where a double blue marker indicates a left turn for the trail. You continue beside the stream, which is below on your right with lovely vignettes of water and the shingle-filled gully. The pleasant walk continues as you cross the stream, where you see a small waterfall over rock ledges uphill on your left and a slag heap from another bluestone mine on your right. About thirty-five minutes after you leave Cat Hollow Road, your trail again intersects a woods road. Turn left on it, and

continue climbing. After another five minutes you see the Campbell Mountain lean-to on your left, a good spot for a lunch break.

The long curving walk uphill continues, relieved with foam flowers, Dutchman's-breeches, violets, white as snow on the trail, and blue cohosh against the blue-stone ledges. Have you noticed how profuse are the wild flowers on the damp

northern slopes of the mountains you have climbed, how sparse they are on the dryer southern slopes? After twenty minutes, you reach a height of land, sensing only a deep valley, left and through the trees, but with no views. The unnamed mountain that is next on this walk also is barely visible through the foliage. The continuing route is a traverse across to the head of the valley for a short descent into it. After you angle across the ridge, you zigzag back left, to continue downhill on a beautifully built old roadway that was carved into the side of the hill. At the bottom, beyond an open field, you reach Campbell Brook Road, a dirt road, at a point high in the valley.

Turn left on the road, and shortly you see a guideboard that gives Russell Brook Road as 5.4 miles distant. The blue-marked trail continues through an open field with views of the mountain ahead and the ridge you just traversed on the mountain behind. Left, off the woods road, there is a picnic table and campsite. Here you turn left to cross the stream and continue sharply uphill on the abandoned road. After a fifteen-minute climb, your route intersects another woods road, and here you turn left away from another bluestone quarry. A forty-minute walk brings you to a second road crossing, where here again you turn left. The sign here is wrong, for you are now on the Trout Pond Trail, 2.5 miles from

that pond's lean-to.

Each section of trail you have walked today has its special points. This one begins at a bridge over a small stream where the road turns to follow the stream through a lovely hemlock grove with bluestone ledges above the trail. A second bridge takes you over a small stream that tumbles with little waterfalls from the mountainside on your left. The walk becomes more steep, following the roadway that is now dished out and rubbly from wear. About half an hour's climb takes you to another gently rounded summit with a guideboard indicating mileages on the route you have just followed.

The descent, through a tall stand of shagbark hickory, soon yields views of Trout Pond. There is a lean-to to the right of the trail intersection at the shore. You could turn right here, past the lean-to, to Mud Pond, two miles distant, for a longer, 3.2-mile walk back to Russell Brook. Considering the distance you have already traveled, you may wish to turn left for the 1.4-mile return walk.

This is the only section of trail on which you are likely to see other hikers. The walk beside the pond, which has a second lean-to at its southern end, bears the tracks of recent vehicular use. You quickly leave the shores of the long thin lake and continue gently downhill. The Mud Pond trail comes in on the right, and you parallel the point outlet to a field beside Russell Brook. Here, for one more treat, walk up along that brook to enjoy its lovely waterfalls. Your car is a hundred yards farther along the trail.

Dry Brook Ridge

Distance: 7 miles
Time: 4½ hours
Vertical rise: 2,000 feet
Map: NY–NJTC Catskill Trails Map #42

The Dry Brook Ridge Trail provides a short but fairly strenuous outing that will give you a look at the scenic valley of the Delaware's east branch, Cold Spring Hollow, and the long line of Mill Brook Ridge.

The trail has three access points. The Mill Brook Road trailhead, which is the longest access, is also the ridge's busiest, being close to both the Mill Brook and Dry Brook Ridge lean-tos. This southerly access to the ridge is also where the northerly access to Balsam Lake and Graham Mountains is located, just uphill of Furlough Lake, which flows east into Dry Brook and north to join the Bush Kill in Arkville. Both creeks drain into the Delaware.

The westernmost access is located in Margaretville, where the trail crosses the Pakatakan Mountain for the 9.4-mile ridge hike. Still another, which is the shortest and most interesting approach, is the yellow trail through German Hollow.

The German Hollow Trail begins at the end of Soderling Road, a short dirt dead end that you'll find 0.25 mile south of Arkville off Dry Brook Road. Arkville itself is on NY 28 west of Kingston, between Margaretville and Fleischmanns.

Don't be fooled into thinking that you'll save a thousand feet of elevation by beginning the hike at the Mill Brook Road trailhead; you will make up for it in the undulating terrain of the ridge, while covering a good deal more distance.

Follow 0.25 mile to the end of Soderling Road, where the trail starts at a parking lot and runs between German Hollow and Reservoir Hollow to join the ridge trail. You begin immediately uphill over a rough jeep trail, encountering the trail register on your left. Continue uphill, passing a long, crumbling stone wall on your left, and climb through a pleasant hemlock grove.

Within a half-hour you will reach the German Hollow lean-to, where the trail switches back nearly 180 degrees. Located in a stand of tall, thin ash, the lean-to provides no view, but it has a sturdy stone fireplace, a good roof and wooden floor, and a nearby spring that produces even in dry weather. You can find the spring by walking directly out of the lean-to and down a short spur trail for a hundred yards.

As you continue your ascent from the

Dry Brook Valley

© 1983 New York–New Jersey Trail Conference

lean-to, within fifteen minutes you reach another spring, marked by a tall cairn on the trail's right side. By now the forest cover is predominantly hardwood, as it will remain for the rest of the hike. The trail is self-guiding and well-marked, over a combination of mineral soil and broken stone.

Once you reach the junction of the German Hollow and Dry Brook Ridge trails, which is not much more than a twenty-five minute hike from the lean-to, you'll see several trail signs. Follow to the left on the blue trail in the direction of Mill Brook Road. You won't be going the entire 6.35 miles to the road, however. The views are located at elevations of 3300 and 3400 feet, at the ridge's summit, which is two miles ahead.

The trail is flat for a stretch until it returns to its old tricks, running steeply up and down for twenty minutes, then leveling out through ledgy terrain and some wet areas where the trail can be soft. You'll walk through a consistent distribution of beech, birch, and maple, with a corresponding appearance of moosewood, pin cherry, choke cherry, hop hornbeam, hobblebush, oxalis, woodfern, viburnum, blackberry, raspberry, and blueberry.

After climbing another ledge, you will reach a boulder with limited views and, following it, weaving in and out of trees along the western ridge line, you will at last reach a 150-foot long exposed outcropping with lots of blueberry bushes and some fine views to the west. As you look straight out into the valley you will see Cold Spring Hollow directly below you, with its Huckleberry Brook reaching for the Delaware. To the left, beyond Mill Brook Valley, is the long Mill Brook Ridge, running east-west from the vicinity of Woodpecker Ridge and the unseen Balsam Lake Mountain. You can see the Delaware's east branch as it flows from Margaretville and into the Pepacton Reservoir, a New York City water supply reservoir that is known for producing record brown trout.

You are at the Ridge's summit, and although one or two more views are available to the west, they are lesser versions of the same westerly exposure. Regrettably there are no views to the east.

Delaware County is a highly scenic and heavily farmed setting of low, gently sculpted hills spotted with rich cultivated fields and long vistas. It has over 900 miles of trout streams, has led New York State from time to time in the annual deer harvest, and supports native populations of wild turkey, grouse, woodcock, and snowshoe hare.

While in Arkville you should take advantage of the Delaware and Ulster Rail Ride, which runs from Arkville to Fleischmanns and Highmount. Railroads came to the Arkville area in 1871, fostering the great resort boom that followed. Riding the "Red Heifer," (a combination diesel, mail, freight, and passenger car called a brill) through this scenic territory will give you appreciation for the easterly upper Delaware Valley that cannot be seen from the heights of Dry Brook Ridge.

(For more information on the rail ride, write Delaware & Hudson, P.O. Box 243, Stamford, N.Y. 12167.)

Balsam Lake Mountain Loop

Distance: 6 miles
Time: 4½ hours
Vertical rise: 1,123 feet
Map: NY–NJTC Catskill Trails Map #42

Balsam Lake Mountain and Graham Mountain are sister peaks, in the southwestern-central Catskills. Many hikers, particularly those wishing to join the Catskill 3500 Club, bag both Balsam Lake and Graham in a single outing. The hiker not tallying peaks might avoid Graham because of its one serious drawback: the view is limited unless you climb the old concrete and steel frame of an abandoned microwave station. Including Graham in this outing adds another three miles to the hike, lengthening the total distance to nine miles and involving an additional 620 feet of vertical rise.

The views from Balsam Lake's fire tower, on the other hand, make the trip a worthwhile one for both peak-baggers and touring hikers, many of whom you'll encounter on the trail during a sunny weekend. If you feel energetic, climb both.

To reach Balsam Lake Mountain, go in from the north, off Mill Brook Road. From Arkville, find Dry Brook Road (County Route 49), which leaves NY 28 and heads south. From 28, go six miles south on Dry Brook Road, straight through Mapledale to Mill Brook Road. Take Mill Brook Road to the right, and go uphill 2.3 miles, where you will find the well-

marked trailhead on your left. Blue trail signs here indicate directions to the Balsam Lake Mountain fire tower, the lean-to (there are two), and Claryville. Be sure you take this trail, not the one on the north (or right) side of the road that crosses Dry Brook Ridge.

You will find the first section of trail easy to hike and legally driveable; however, only four-wheel drive vehicles should attempt it, and the road is barricaded before the summit is reached. Immediately you'll notice a forest of beech, birch, maple, and cherry over cinnamon ferns, oxalis, and viburnum. In five minutes you will reach the trail register on your left.

Follow along through a flat section of the trail, which is paralleled by the fire tower and observer's cabin telephone lines, to an uphill section that allows occasional views across Mill Brook Hollow to the west. Ascend gently through a few switchbacks, which can be seen on the map. Look for trailside specimens of jack-in-the-pulpit, Solomon's seal, wolf's claw club moss, and haircap moss. The upright, branched, and densely leaved stems of wolf's claw club moss are used commercially for Christmas decorations. (Picking them in the Preserve is pro-

© 1983 New York–New Jersey Trail Conference

hibited.) The moss is widely distributed through the Catskills and northern North America. It can be confused with the similarly distributed tree club moss, or ground pine, which is usually found in open pine woods and bogs.

In ten minutes or so you will see a good spring to the right and downhill (indicated by a sign) among a series of sedimentary boulders, many of which are covered with rock tripe. When soaked for several weeks in water, this lichen renders a purple dye that has some popularity among textile artisans. It is also edible, if not entirely wholesome. The dried-up, curled disks of lichen resemble very moldy potato chips. Eat them if you must, but remember that it is

illegal (and immoral) to remove any plant life from the forest preserve.

In another twenty minutes you pass a grass-covered trail on your left that leads to Graham's summit. In a few moments you encounter several trail signs. Take the red trail to your right, which goes to Balsam Lake Mountain fire tower (0.85 mile). At this point a sign prohibits entry of any motorized vehicles.

Continue going uphill over flat rocks where glacial scratches can be seen. The trail includes some vigorous ascents broken up by more moderate inclines, hedged in blackberry, bunchberry, and spruce fir thickets.

After twenty minutes of continually thinking that each rise will produce the

Balsam Lake Mountain and Graham Mountain

summit, you at last see the fire tower and observer's cabin come into view. Climb to the top of the tower (without which there would be no view), where you can see in all directions. Below the tower, and running north, is the Dry Brook Ridge. To the northeast on a clear day you can see as far as Bearpen Mountain, fifteen miles away. Closer at hand is the ridge on the east side of the Dry Brook Valley and its series of peaks. From left to right are the masses of Belleayre, Balsam, Haynes, Eagle, and Big Indian. Between the latter two, the summit of Panther can be seen. Due east of you is the

range that includes Slide and Table. The two neighboring peaks are Graham and Doubletop. To the south and west are the rolling, seemingly endless lower peaks of Delaware County, which includes some of the most sparsely populated lands within the Catskill Park.

Just off the summit, in an impenetrable tangle of blowdown, is a unique plant community: a bog. Researchers call this bog unique because it contains more sphagnum than other bogs in the Catskill region. A hurricane on November 25, 1950, caused extensive blowdown in the northeast half of the bog, which was followed by a heavy second growth of balsam fir. It has been hypothesized that this bog may never follow a bog's normal growth pattern, because of the infiltration of acid rain, which acts to decompose peat. Water is retained, and the bog stage remains rather than progresses. Balsam Lake summit recently has been the site of acid rain studies, a question that has come of age in the Catskills, despite the profusion of its limestone, which acts to buffer acids.

The trail continues downhill past an outbuilding with signs indicating the lean-to at 0.45 mile. Follow downhill, passing an open primitive campsite with a fire ring on your right. You will see a lean-to on your left shortly thereafter; it's in rough shape, with a dirt floor. A more inviting lean-to is beyond it to the east. It is in much better shape, with a wooden floor and an interesting quarter-loft for stowing packs and possibly sleeping. Views to the south are available here beyond the lean-tos.

Descend toward the blue trail, passing a spring just below the lean-to area, and within twenty minutes you intersect with the blue trail once again. Go left in the direction of Mill Brook lean-to, and follow this pleasant, grassy road uphill for twenty minutes to the junction of the main trail to Balsam Lake Mountain (blue). Ten minutes ahead of you is the grassy trail to Graham, which is unmarked but obvious on map #42. If you wish to take it, descend slightly, reaching the intersection in ten minutes, and go right. The trail heads uphill from here, and brings you to the summit in about forty minutes. Although it is easily followed, the trail is not well maintained, and should the thick overhanging boughs and bushes become wet, so will you.

While Graham's summit provides only a limited view into Dry Brook Hollow, the view from atop the concrete television transmitting building (now a shameful mess) is equal to and perhaps better than that from Balsam Lake Mountain. You see the patchwork of farms and hedgerows of Dry Brook Valley, whose shading and brilliance is much like what we see for October calendar pictures entitled "Vermont." As if such beauty only existed there!

The next peak is Doubletop, with its balsam fir and spruce-covered twin summits, looking foreboding and desolate on a dark afternoon. Beyond Doubletop, still to the east, the peaks running between Slide and Table are clearly visible. Peaks of Cornell and Wittenberg can be seen to Slide's left and, of course, there are southerly valley vistas. But it is the view down into Dry Brook Valley that makes the trip worth the extra effort.

From the trail junction of the Balsam Lake Mountain and Graham trail, you are fifty minutes from your starting point on Mill Brook Road.

Bear Pen Mountain

Distance: 6.5 miles
Time: 5 hours
Vertical rise: 1,600 feet
Map: USGS 7½′ Prattsville; NYSDT Prattsville

Bear Pen gets little attention from hikers because it is outside the Catskill Park, is not a state-marked or maintained trail, and is seldom discussed in books or by hikers other than those of the Catskill 3500 Club.

The trail is an easy but uneventful walk until you reach the summit, where long views of the Schoharie Valley and the Delaware County farmlands make the long jeep road hike worthwhile.

John Burroughs looked upon the western slopes of Bear Pen from Boyhood Rock in Roxbury, where he was born in 1837. He is buried near Boyhood Rock, and his summer home, Woodchuck Lodge, which you can visit on the same day you climb Bear Pen, can be seen from the road and is open to the public during summer months. Boyhood Rock is a short hike into the fields. Both places can be visited in less than an hour once you get to Roxbury.

To reach Bear Pen, follow NY 23A until just east of Prattsville, where County Route 2 goes south. Turn here, and immediately cross the Schoharie Creek over an old iron bridge. Once across the creek turn right, and bear right at the first fork you encounter a short distance ahead. Within a mile of the bridge, bear left, following uphill over a paved road, turning away from the creek. After 1.2 miles, go right at the T (left is a dead end). In another 1.9 miles of scenic driving, with Bear Pen and Vly Mountains visible on your left (south) you will reach an intersection where you continue on County Route 2. (Straight ahead at this intersection, one-eighth of a mile west on a dead end, is a cemetery that is shown on the USGS map. This will help you identify your location.)

Turn right at this intersection where the road climbs uphill for 0.6 mile, passing another cemetery on the right, and reaching a jeep trail on your left at the crest of the hill. This is the trailhead. Parking is available here in a grove of maple trees where you can look south-southwest at Bear Pen's summit and its abandoned ski lodge, your destination.

Start hiking on an easy road that ascends consistently, passing stone walls on the left and right. In ten minutes you will reach state land (you have been hiking a public easement), where several blue paint blazes run everywhere but along the trail. The road is so good that it

Bear Pen Mountain

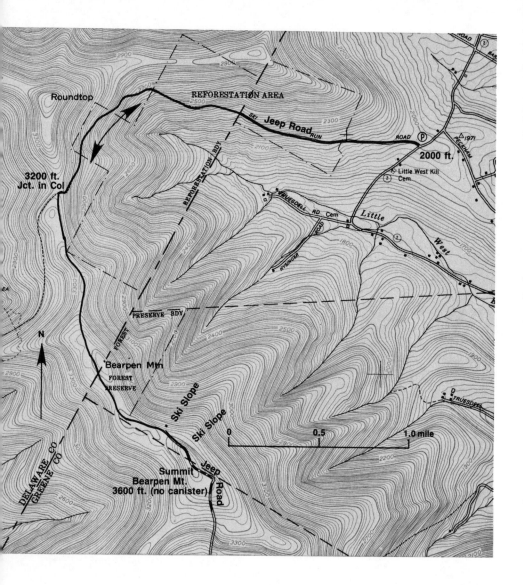

needs no marking. Except for occasional deep mud puddles along its upper elevations, the entire road to the ski lodge is driveable but is not open to the public.

Because of this, the trail is relatively featureless and not terribly exciting, but you will see a profusion of white violets, jack-in-the-pulpit, spring beauties, rue anemone, and Dutchman's breeches, which may take the edge off your impatience. You also will be serenaded by what seems an unusually high population of songbirds. The ovenbirds will cry "teacher, teacher" as you try to locate them. Rose-breasted grosbeaks and phoebes will flit curiously above as you walk. Myrtle warblers and red-winged blackbirds will betray themselves amid the green leaves of popple and maple.

In forty-five minutes or more of this steady incline, with only occasional views through trees to the east, you reach a junction where a road leads right to Roundtop (3200 feet). Bear left, toward Bear Pen. You are walking south now, through blackberry patches, where the trail is literally lined with spring beauties in early season. Within thirty-five minutes of the junction to Roundtop you will reach a flat, open area where the summit is visible ahead of you. Shortly thereafter you reach the ski lodge and pond. From here the summit ridge is still ahead, up a short, steep incline. There isn't much of interest around the old ski lodge, which is now a disastrous eyesore. The area closed because of access difficulties, and the building subsequently was vandalized.

Once you reach the summit ridge, the actual summit is ahead of you. From various points on the summit and its approach, Utsayantha can be seen to the west, as well as (from right to left on the southerly exposure) Balsam Lake, Graham, Doubletop, and the Highmount and Belleayre ski areas (left to right, respectively). Continue going east until you reach more ski trails, the second of which approximates the summit.

Bear Pen's summit is deciduous, predominantly maple, birch, and cherry. On the ski slopes facing north you will find platforms of several old lifts, which were powered by old automobiles whose carcasses appear here and there. The views to the north and east are good, mostly consisting of low, nameless peaks, parts of the Schoharie Reservoir near West Conesville, and as far east as Windham High Peak and Thomas Cole Mountain in the Blackhead Range.

It was here, inspired by the expansive terrain beyond, that Bleecker Staats, number 272 of the Catskill 3500 Club, recited his memorable insights on the Catskills, his favorite "movable feast:"

"You can taste it," he began. "You can hear it; its birds moving and singing in the trees. Its breezes; its streams falling over rocks. You can feel it—the surface of the trees, the hair cap moss; you can smell it in the herb green fields, the summit ferns; in its balm of Gilead, and in the pines. You hear the barred owl at night, the scarlet tanager by day, the haunting white throated sparrow."

Below to the northeast is Prattsville, which you might want to visit for no other reason than to see the amazing sculptures at Pratt's Rocks, a short hike from the road. Zadock Pratt was a tanlord, one of, if not the, most successful and influencial tanners in America. His story is told in stone by a series of carvings cut by a journeyman stonecutter whom Pratt befriended. Many of the carvings are larger than life. There is a bust of Zadock Pratt, a hemlock tree and horse, and a likeness of the tannery building he finished in 1824. Beneath this an inscription reads, "One million sides of sole leather tanned with hemlock bark, in twenty years, by Zadock Pratt." A roadside visitors' booth explains the family history and further exploits of this remarkable man. The sculptures are set in vertical rock walls above a visitors' picnic area.

You can visit both the John Burroughs memorial and Pratt's Rocks in the same day that you visit Bear Pen, if you get an early start on the mountain. Consult your map for directions. An understanding of both men's contributions to the area's economy and culture will add immeasurably to your appreciation of the western Catskills.

Belleayre Mountain

Distance: 5 miles
Time: 4 hours
Vertical rise: 1,175 feet
Map: NY–NJTC Catskill Trails Map #42

One of the easiest and most scenic approaches to Belleayre Mountain is via Cathedral Glen, a tricky-to-locate trail running from Pine Hill south to the summit. Pine Hill is a scenic, quiet little community between Big Indian and Highmount on NY 28.

The Rondout and Oswego was the first railroad to penetrate as far as Pine Hill, but only after serious controversies over its construction. Some argued that the railroad from Kingston would threaten the livelihoods of teamsters. On July 4, 1866, the Kingston *Argus* wrote that the road would "strike ruinously at our wagon-makers, our blacksmiths, our harness makers, our flour and feed establishments, our merchants and dealers generally."

The opposite point of view was held by tanners and businessmen along the proposed route, who could see only profit in railroad development. In any case, in 1870, the Rondout and Oswego opened for passenger service as far west as Mount Pleasant. The line later changed hands and took the name of Delaware & Ulster in 1875. Part of the same line can be traveled today via the Delaware & Ulster Rail Ride, which runs west of Pine Hill from Arkville to Highmount.

The railroad's passage through Pine Hill presented some engineering challenges, which resulted in the double horseshoe curve that you see on the map just west of the Cathedral Glen Trail. Prior to the curve's construction, the idea of tunneling through the mountain was popular, but a grant authorized by the legislature was vetoed by then Governor Hoffman.

One of the more ambitious offshoots of the Delaware & Ulster was the Grand Hotel, which the railroad built and owned. Opened in the same year as the Kaaterskill Hotel (1881), the Grand was positioned in Highmount, on the Delaware and Ulster County line, with views of both the Catskills' highest mountains and the lower pasturelands of Delaware County. Proprietors of the Grand, located in two towns and counties, had the unusual power to move both the barroom and hotel office when liquor and tax laws made such moves profitable. The hotel was noted for Diamond Spring, which was praised for its wholesomeness and purity by the hotel's management—and recommended by its physician.

While Arnold Guyot was hurriedly elevating the Shandaken Mountains from little-known peaks to the very tallest of

Catskill summits, the Grand Hotel was busy promoting itself. This shifted considerable attention from the erstwhile nucleus of the Catskills: Pine Orchard and the Catskill Mountain House.

In Pine Hill on NY 28, turn west at the bus stop and then right on Main Street. Several hundred feet ahead, go left on Bonnie View Road. In another few hundred feet or more you will see a state trail sign on Mill Street. Cross a small creek, continue on a dirt road, go under a railroad bridge and take the first right, into an open area. Park here, where the railway bed slips into the woods going west.

You will hike along the abandoned railway bed of the original Rondout and Oswego to come out on the trail that ends on Mill Street (Pine Hill-West Branch Trail). There are no trail signs along the tracks at this point. You still have a ten- or fifteen-minute walk to a small pond on your left, where on the far side there is a shed belonging to the Belleayre Mountain State Ski Center. The pond is shown on the map at the trailhead. On the east

side of the pond the trail departs from the tracks and heads uphill to the south. You may have to look around for a few minutes in order to find the blue trail markers, which follow along the eastern ridge of the bowl created by the pond excavation. These blue trail markers (there is no trail sign) lead to an easily walked jeep road beneath an overstory of large hemlock.

Travel through this climax forest of hemlock, the spires of which may well have inspired the name "Cathedral Glen," and within five minutes the trail will assume the character of a footpath. Shortly you will enter a hardwood forest. After another twenty minutes you reach an open field with a snow fence erected along its edges. You are at the bottom of a ski trail. The trail markers continue uphill, placed sparingly on trees to your left. Keep an eye on the blue disks, for suddenly you will reach an ease in the trail where another ski trail goes off to the right. Look to your left and you will see the blue trail going into the woods in an easterly direction.

Belleayre Mountain

Be glad you can avoid climbing the steep ski trail ahead of you. The wooded trail, which is much gentler, will bring you to the red Belleayre Ridge Trail in ten minutes or so. When you reach the red trail, the ski slopes are to your right and the summit is to your left. Go right at least as far as the lean-to, which will take you only five minutes. There is a view here—and there are more views farther to the west from the ski trails. The aspect is always north and east from the ski trails, with long views including North Dome, Sherrill, Balsam, Halcott, Rose, and Monka Hill. But rather than hiking to

the westerly ski trails of the Belleayre Ski area, you could go directly to the fire tower with its superior views. Although the tower is closed to the public, it still can be safely climbed to just beneath the observation deck.

The hike to the summit from the lean-to takes about fifteen minutes. The terrain is flat over a service road. On the deciduous summit there is a picnic table and fireplace and a group of trail signs. At this junction the Pine Hill–West Branch Trail departs for Balsam, Haynes, and Big Indian Mountains and the Neversink Valley. To your left the Lost Clove Trail goes to Big Indian, intersecting a short way down with the Pine Hill–West Branch Trail's northern leg, which you will take back to Woodchuck Hollow Road and the clearing where your car is parked.

The view from the fire tower is a 360-degree panorama of peaks, including Overlook, Slide, Balsam Lake, Graham, Haynes, Eagle, Doubletop, Panther, Garfield, North Dome, Sherrill, Balsam, and Halcott, and many more mountains and lesser peaks for which you would need Guyot himself to identify. To the northwest you see the gently receding hills of the Delaware Valley.

A short way down the Lost Clove Trail on your left is a lean-to with a latrine on the opposite side of the trail. In less time than it took you to get from the summit to the lean-to (about fifteen minutes), you will reach the blue trail again, where you turn left, descending on an easy road bed, in twenty minutes entering an obvious logged-over area with private postings. The owner has granted an easement here to allow the hiking public to cross these lands. Pass a large logging "deck"—an area where tree-length logs are dragged by a skidder to be loaded onto trucks for transporting. The hike out from here is flat and easy, leading you to a paved road, past the dump on your left, and back to the parking area.

**North of
the Catskills**

214 *North of the Catskills*

49

Vroman's Nose

Distance: 2 miles
Time: 1 hour
Vertical rise: 760 feet
Map: USGS 7½' Middleburgh

The Nose is a trip you save for a lazy afternoon when you'd rather watch than walk. From this geologically unique cliff, 600 feet above the Schoharie Valley, there are fine views of the lowlands and the long ridge of the northern Catskills.

You won't have to work too hard to visit Vroman's Nose, and the hike itself is very easy. It may be harder to find the trailhead. At this writing it had only recently been opened to public use, but it should be better marked by the time you make your visit. Vroman's Nose is west of Middleburgh, which is about one-half hour southwest of the Albany-Schenectady area, at the intersection of NY 30 and 145.

Just south of Middleburgh on NY 30, at 0.6 mile on the right, is Middleburgh Road, which runs into West Middleburgh. Vroman's Nose is obvious; its vertical cliffs rise above NY 30 in front of you. The trail starts north of the hill, to your right as you look south at the Nose. Turn right on Middleburgh Road, and go 0.6 mile to a point where Line Creek crosses the road (the town line between Middleburgh and Fulton). A few hundred feet

Vroman's Nose

beyond the bridge, park on your left, where you'll notice a rough parking area with room for several cars.

A wagon road runs south through a hayfield from here, into a forest of large pine and hemlock, turning right as it leaves the field. The path is self-guiding, and a steady climb over easy terrain (steep in places) will take you through a hardwood forest to the "summit." You actually can cover the distance in twenty minutes, but take your time to enjoy the views of the Catskills that will open up toward the south. The overlook, a long and dangerous cliff, is located approximately fifty feet southeast of the summit, a wooded plateau of roughly ten acres.

The heavily scored summit of Hamilton sandstone shows evidence of its past in the scratches (*striae*) and chatter marks of a retreating glacier, which moved from the northeast about 50,000 years ago, forming the present topography of the Schoharie Valley. The cliff is heavily engraved with initials and ugly painted graffiti, to such a point that it has an erosive effect. Fortunately, there is very little litter surrounding the few crude fireplaces people have assembled nearby.

Trees such as oak, hickory, pine, and cedar thrive on the plateau, which is covered in bearberry (called *kinikinick* by the Indians). The early spring flower, fringed polygala, also appears.

Dr. Vincent J. Schaefer comments on the presence of brachiopods, pelycepods, and trilobites that characterizes the Middle Devonian-period thin sheets of Hamilton sandstone. Flagstones from Vroman's Nose were used for sidewalks in cities such as Troy, Albany, and Schenectady.

Early in 1942 Dr. Schaefer visited the Nose while an employee of the General Electric Research Laboratory to photograph the testing of artificial fog generators, ultimately used for the screening of ships, personnel, and cities from air attack during World War II. He pointed out a curious atmospheric phenomenon that generates a strong thermal updraft against the cliff:

"The dark-colored rocks of the cliffs of Hamilton shale and sandstone become quite warm whenever the sun is shining on them. This produces a massive up-

current of heated air. Light objects such as grass, small twigs and similar objects when thrown away from the cliff edge are carried upward and toward the north."

You may notice birds, notably turkey buzzards, taking advantage of this free ride. This presents an opportunity to get some good pictures of them as they circle lazily out of sight with no wing movement.

The long, open fields of farmland to the north, east, and south of Vroman's Nose were settled originally by Indians, who have left evidence of campfires under its thin soils. It was a Schenectady farmer, Adam Vroman, who established the first farm here in 1713. He was followed by German palatines who originally settled in the lower Hudson River Valley. Crops common to the valley today are corn and carrots. In the past, hops were grown successfully in the alluvial flats along the Schoharie.

Dr. Schaefer originally conceived of the

Long Path in 1931, then planned to cross Vroman's Nose. The Path's purpose is the same today as then: to link the outstanding scenic, geological, prehistoric, and historic features of the area traversed.

Beginning at the George Washington Bridge in New York City and ending in the northern Adirondacks at Whiteface Mountain, the Path comes up from Gilboa, following old roads on the valley's east side. From Keyser Kill Falls through Panther Creek to Brouck Falls, and into the high country beyond Fultonham and Watsonville, it follows hill roads near Patria and then descends the ridge to Vroman's Nose. From there it drops down to cross the Schoharie at Middleburgh, goes east through the village, follows a woods road to the top of a rocky cliff east of town, and heads for Dutch Billy's Hill in the Helderbergs.

Although its founders originally intended to construct Adirondack-type lean-to shelters a day's hike apart along the Path, these ambitious plans were interrupted by World War II. The Long Path still has its enthusiasts, however, whose mission it is to maintain and continue the trail to its planned destination.

Those who have walked sections of the Long Path may have been frustrated by the sparingly applied blue blaze that designates it. Unlike present hiking trails, the trail originally was meant to be unmarked except on topographic maps. "Thus," to quote Dr. Schaefer, "a hiker most know how to read a topographic map. Such a route eliminates most of the difficulties of trail maintenance and marking, over-use, litter, and the host of other problems that are inherent in the present trail systems. The Schoharie Valley and especially the Vroman's Nose area is a perfect example of the Long Path idea."

Looking south you will have fine views of Windham High Peak and the Blackhead Range, beyond long esplanades of furrowed ground, a geographical contrast that is as unique as Vroman's Nose itself.

Thacher and Indian Ladder

Distance: 0.5 mile
Time: 45 minutes
Vertical rise: Insignificant
Map: USGS 7½' Altamont

Indian Ladder is a short walk, best enjoyed along with a picnic to John Boyd Thacher Park and strolls through its lovely grounds, which cap the Helderberg Escarpment. The trail, less than half a mile long, explores one of the state's most striking geological formations; here is a wonderful place to view the accumulations of sand and lime-mud that have been compressed into rock, uplifted, and eroded to form the mountain bastions bordering the plains that much later became the site of the sea of Albany. These light-colored ramparts derive their name from the Dutch, *helder*, meaning bright or light, and *berg*, meaning mountain.

The uplift of these mountains in the Early Tertiary and later glacial actions expose a long segment of the earth's history, so a trip to study these formations makes an informative outing. Combine it with the view from the amphitheater formed by the cliffs or a picnic beneath the shade trees of the Paint Mine or Indian Ladder picnic areas, and you have a day in a pastoral setting unlike any that exists in the lowlands before you.

This is a nice getaway spot for a lazy summer afternoon when you are not quite up to a strenuous hike. Be warned,

though, as weekends here can be very crowded. The park is easily reached from the capitol district. Coming west from Albany from NY 20, take NY 146 into Altamont where NY 156 branches to the right. Follow 156 to the junction of NY 157 and a sign pointing left to the park, five miles distant. There is plenty of parking. You will find good directions to the trailhead, whose starting point is just north of the Indian Ladder picnic area, behind the park's administration building. A comfort station is located here also.

Verplanck Colvin, the surveyor who mapped the wilderness areas of northern New York, wrote about the Helderbergs in 1869, shedding some light on the origin of the name Indian Ladder. "What is this Indian Ladder so often mentioned? In 1710 this Helderberg region was a wilderness; nay all westward of the Hudson River settlement was unknown. Albany was a frontier town, a trading post, a place where annuities were paid, and blankets exchanged with Indians for beaver pelts. From Albany over the sand plains . . . 'Schenectada' (pine barrens) of the Indians . . . led an Indian trail west-

Indian Ladder trail

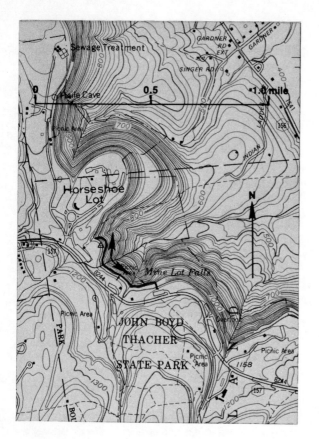

ward. Straight as the wild bee or the crow the wild Indian made his course from the white man's settlement to his own home in the beauteous Schoharie Valley. The stern cliffs of these hills opposed his progress; his hatchet fells a tree against them, the stumps of the branches which he trimmed away formed the round of the Indian Ladder."

While it may be that an old Indian Ladder once leaned against this cliff, it has been replaced by the heavy steel staircases that now serve a curious public. This first section of trail follows what was originally the Indian Ladder road, constructed in 1828 from Albany and west-

ward into the Schoharie Valley.

The upper layers of rock are the youngest known to geologists as the Coeymans Limestone. That formation takes its name from the nearby town where it is well exposed. Of the two limestone formations in Thacher Park, the Coeymans is the thickest, averaging fifty feet from top to bottom. Look closely here and you may find the preserved remains of small sea creatures. These hard shelled fossils of *Sieberella Coeymanensis* and other invertebrates date from the Late Silurian and Lower Devonian periods, about 415 million years ago.

Continuing down the trail you will notice thin layers (two to three inches) of alternating light and dark beds of a "ribbon limestone," which is softer than the Coeymans and recedes beneath it as a result of erosion. This is Manlius Limestone, a formation used extensively in the manufacture of cement at Manlius near Syracuse. Those thin limestone ribbons form a fifty-foot thick layer that also contains the preserved remains of invertebrate sea creatures and algae. Part of the formation also contains a two to three inch layer of waterlime, which has been used for making the Portland cement that will set up underwater. This forms a ledge known in the park as the "Upper Bear Path." At the base of the Manlius formation is limey mudrock known as Rondout Formation. It is a waterlime that is well exposed near the Ulster County town of Rondout. It was used to produce Rosendale, or natural cement. This formation is less resistant to erosion and has eroded back to form the "Lower Bear Path," the ledge you are standing on.

The presence of limestones in Thacher Park, and its characteristic ability to dissolve in rainwater, has caused such phenomena as disappearing streams, sinkholes, caves, and underground streams. The erosion underground can form caves, which occasionally collapse to form surface depressions called sinkholes. The Karst topography is named after its frequent appearance in the Karst region of the Dalmatian Alps. Nearby Thompson's Lake is a sinkhole, which drains through a subterranean cave at its south end.

Once in the large amphitheater, which is called Indian Ladder Gulf, you will see Outley and Minelot Creeks. Together they have been responsible for the erosion of this impressive embayment. When the water table is high, these two creeks form spectacular falls that you can walk behind on the trail. The talus slope beneath the cliff consists of rock that has been broken off and fallen from the cliff face. Along the Indian Ladder Walk, watch for the small, limestone-loving ferns, such as cliffbrakes and spleenworts.

The view from clifftop encompasses the Adirondack foothills, Vermont's Green Mountains, the Berkshires of western Massachusetts, and the Taconics. There are paths at clifftop with views or shaded paths behind that you can follow to extend the forty-five minute walk along the Indian Ladder into a fair day's outing.

Guidebooks from The Countryman Press and Backcountry Publications

Written for people of all ages and experience, these popular and carefully prepared books feature detailed trail and tour directions, notes on points of interest and natural phenomena, maps and photographs.

Walks and Rambles Series

Walks and Rambles on the Delmarva Peninsula $8.95
Walks and Rambles in Westchester (NY) and Fairfield (CT) Counties $7.95
Walks and Rambles in Rhode Island $8.95

Biking Series

25 Bicycle Tours in New Jersey $8.95
25 Bicycle Tours in Delmarva $8.95
25 Bicycle Tours in Maine $8.95
25 Bicycle Tours in Vermont $7.95
25 Bicycle Tours in New Hampshire $6.95
20 Bicycle Tours in the Finger Lakes $7.95
20 Bicycle Tours in and around New York City $6.95
25 Bicycle Tours in Eastern Pennsylvania $7.95

Canoeing Series

Canoe Camping Vermont and New Hampshire Rivers $6.95
Canoeing Central New York $9.95
Canoeing Massachusetts, Rhode Island and Connecticut $7.95

Hiking Series

50 Hikes in New Jersey $10.95
50 Hikes in the Adirondacks $9.95
50 Hikes in Central New York $8.95
50 Hikes in the Hudson Valley $9.95
50 Hikes in Central Pennsylvania $9.95
50 Hikes in Eastern Pennsylvania $9.95
50 Hikes in Western Pennsylvania $9.95
50 Hikes in Maine $8.95
50 Hikes in the White Mountains $9.95
50 More Hikes in New Hampshire $9.95
50 Hikes in Vermont, 3rd edition $9.95

50 Hikes in Massachusetts $9.95
50 Hikes in Connecticut $8.95
50 Hikes in West Virginia $9.95

Adirondack Series

Discover the Southern Adirondacks $9.95
Discover the South Central Adirondacks $8.95
Discover the Southeastern Adirondacks $8.95
Discover the Central Adirondacks $8.95
Discover the Southwestern Adirondacks $9.95
Discover the Northeastern Adirondacks $9.95
Discover the Eastern Adirondacks $9.95
Discover the West Central Adirondacks $9.95

Ski-Touring Series

25 Ski Tours in Central New York $7.95
25 Ski Tours in Maine $5.95
25 Ski Tours in the Adirondacks $5.95
25 Ski Tours in the White Mountains (revised edition available fall 1988)
25 Ski Tours in Vermont (revised edition available fall 1988)

Other Guides

State Parks and Campgrounds in Northern New York $9.95
The Complete Boating Guide to the Connecticut River $9.95
The Other Massachusetts: An Explorer's Guide $12.95
Maine: An Explorer's Guide $13.95
Vermont: An Explorer's Guide, 3rd edition (spring 1988)
New England's Special Places $10.95
New York's Special Places (spring 1988)

The above titles are available at bookstores and at certain sporting goods stores or may be ordered directly from the publisher. For complete descriptions of these and other guides, write: The Countryman Press, P.O. Box 175, Woodstock, VT 05091.